Our Foreign-Born Citizens

Our
Foreign-Born
Citizens

NEW REVISED EDITION

By *Annie E. S. Beard*

Revised by William A. Fahey

THOMAS Y. CROWELL COMPANY
NEW YORK

920
Bea

LIBRARY OF CONGRESS CATALOG CARD NO. 55-9203

Twenty-fifth Printing
(Seventh Printing of Fifth Edition)

Manufactured in the United States of America by
the Vail-Ballou Press, Inc., Binghamton, New York

Preface

MOST Americans are immigrants or the descendants of immigrants. The American Indian alone can safely trace all the roots of his family tree back to their source in the soil of America. And scholars tell us that even the Indian probably immigrated in prehistoric times, coming into the western hemisphere over a land bridge that once connected the Americas with Asia. Unfortunately, people whose families have lived in this country for two, three, four, or more generations sometimes tend to forget these facts. They assume that length of stay has given them certain privileges—certain virtues even—which later comers cannot share. Nothing, of course, could be further from the truth. Early comers and late, all have contributed to the greatness of America, and all must share in its privileges if our country is to remain a great one.

From the time of its first printing, one of the great values of *Our Foreign-Born Citizens* has been its demonstration of the importance of the role that immigrants have played in developing our country. But since Miss Beard wrote her book there have been many more newcomers to America. And these newcomers have made important contributions, too. New industries have sprung up, and immigrants like Igor Sikorsky, Spyros Skouras and Raymond Loewy have risen with them. Walter Gropius has fostered a new school of architecture. New leadership has been demanded by our workers, and men like Philip Murray have answered the call. Our stage has been graced with a new dignity in the person of Judith Anderson. Popular entertainment has been provided by people like Alfred Hitchcock, from England, and Russian-born Irving Berlin, both unknown to Miss Beard. Since her day, too, American art has been enriched by the work of George Grosz, a painter who fled to America to escape Nazi oppression. And the frontiers of darkness have been pushed further back through the efforts of Dr. Hideyo Noguchi, a Japanese-born scientist of genius.

America has profited enormously from the work of her immigrants. But she has not always been uniformly just in her treatment of these her benefactors. Hideyo Noguchi never became a citizen of the United States, though he wished to become one. Prejudicial laws enacted by bigoted legislators discriminated against members of his race for many years, denying them citizenship. Dr. Noguchi appears in this book because he was a great American;

Preface

that he was not technically a citizen was no fault of his.

One further word must be said about Miss Beard's work. Rectifying an injustice, she brought recognition to American citizens of foreign birth whose contributions to our country had long been overlooked. In doing so she did a service for the immigrant and for her country. Of course, with the passage of time new information on some of her subjects has come to light. In some cases, notably the chapters on Andrew Carnegie and Angelo Patri, this information has been significant enough to justify a reassessment of the subject. But in the majority of instances I have merely supplemented what Miss Beard had to say by adding information which she did not have access to when she wrote.

WILLIAM A. FAHEY

Contents

Contents

Our Foreign-Born Citizens

John James Audubon

"THE king of ornithological painters" was the flattering salutation given on October 1, 1828, by the great Italian painter Gerard to John James Audubon, after a review of his wonderful life-size drawings of the birds of America. Baron Cuvier, a noted Frenchman, spoke of them as "the most splendid monuments which art has erected in honor of ornithology."

The man who won this high praise was born in the Louisiana territory on May 4, 1780. He was a Frenchman, all his ancestors being French except his mother, who was Spanish. His father was the twentieth child of a poor fisherman in the Department of Vendee, in France. At the early age of twelve he set out to seek his fortune and became a sailor. Finally he was given command of a small vessel of the Imperial navy and frequently visited America. So it happened that his famous son, John James, was born there, although a few years later he was taken to the home at Nantes, in France.

He spent a happy boyhood, for through his stepmother's indulgence he was not kept strictly at school but was allowed to spend much time in the woods watching the birds and gathering their nests, thus early showing the interest which became the dominant influence of his life. His father, on his return home from a voyage, finding the boy was missing the benefits of an education, sent him away to school. Among other studies he had the advantage of drawing lessons from the celebrated painter, David, from whom he learned how to sketch from nature. At the age of seventeen he had already made sketches of two hundred varieties of birds, but his father was disappointed in him because he did not wish to serve under Napoleon as a soldier. As an alternative to such service the boy was sent to America to look after some of his father's property at Mill Grove, near the Schuylkill Falls.

At Mill Grove he spent his time hunting, fishing, and drawing. Love at first sight resulted from a visit he made at the home of his next-door neighbor, an Englishman with a beautiful daughter. After an interval of a few years, Audubon married the girl, Miss Lucy Bakewell. Both before and after his marriage various ventures into business ended disastrously. He had no aptitude for a commercial life and devoted himself far more assiduously to outdoor occupations, studying with eagerness the habits of the birds and animals found in the woods. His father's death brought him no financial gain, for the merchant with whom his father had deposited seventeen thousand dollars refused to hand the money over to the son until assured of his legal right to it. Meanwhile the merchant died penniless and John James never recovered any of the money due him. With a singular disregard of his own interests he transferred to his sister Rosa the estate left by his father in France.

Another business venture turning out badly, he commenced portrait-painting. In this he succeeded remarkably well. Soon afterward he was offered the position of curator at a museum in Cincinnati, receiving liberal compensation for his preparation of birds. He also opened a drawing-school in the city and for a while did well financially.

On October 12, 1820, Audubon started on an expedition into Mississippi, Alabama, and Florida, in search of ornithological specimens. His *Journal* gives interesting descriptions of what he saw in his wanderings, and the reader is impressed with his enthusiasm over the birds and their habits. At Natchez he was in need of new shoes, and so also was a fellow traveler. Neither had the money to purchase them, but Audubon went to a shoemaker and offered to make portraits of the man and his wife in return for a new pair of shoes for his traveling companion and himself. The offer was accepted and both men went on their way newly shod.

Upon arriving in New Orleans Audubon sought vainly for employment. He secured a few orders for portraits which relieved his financial need, and he continued his work of painting birds. He also had an engagement to teach drawing at sixty dollars a month for half of each day. Some fourteen months later he sent for his family to join him in New Orleans. He rented a house for seventeen dollars a month and began life again with forty-two dollars. In order to educate the children Mrs. Audubon took a position as governess. Depressed in spirit because of his lack of success in earning money, her husband again went to Natchez, paying his way on the boat by a crayon portrait of the captain and his wife. He taught drawing, music, and French in the family of a Portuguese gentleman, and drawing in a neighboring college.

After various trying experiences Audubon reached Philadelphia in the hope that he might obtain help to complete his work on birds. Through an old friend he was introduced to men of standing and influence, especially the portrait-painter Sully, who aided him greatly by giving him instruction in oil painting. With kind letters of introduction he went next to New York City but, being unsuccessful there also, he went West, mainly subsisting on bread and milk. When he arrived at Bayou Sara he found his wife had earned three thousand dollars which, with wifely generosity, she offered to him to help the publication of his book. He resolved on a new effort to increase the amount and engaged to teach dancing to a class of sixty men and women. This brought him two thousand dollars. His determination to persevere in accomplishing the great wish of his life, in spite of these many hardships, is really remarkable.

Fortunately, at the age of forty-six, the tide of fortune turned and he started for England, where he hoped to win for his book on birds the appreciative help he had failed to find in America. In England he was welcomed cordially. From the exhibition of his pictures in Liverpool he received five hundred dollars. In Edinburgh the Royal Institution offered the use of its rooms for an exhibit which brought in from twenty-five dollars to seventy-five dollars a day. He wrote to his wife:

> My success borders on the miraculous. My book is to be published in numbers, containing four birds in each, the size of life, in a style surpassing anything now existing, at two guineas a number. I am fêted, feasted, elected an honorary member of societies, making money by my exhibition and my paintings.

On March 17, 1827, he issued the prospectus of his book, which was to cost him over one hundred thousand dollars. But his joyous mood could not last long, for hard work and disappointment were still ahead of him. He visited several cities in the endeavor to secure subscribers at one thousand dollars each. Simultaneously he painted pictures and then spent the evenings trying to sell them. He said he never refused any offer made him for these pictures. He often sold five or seven copies of one painting.

Audubon next went to Paris, where he much appreciated the acquaintance of the famous scientist, Baron Cuvier. Among other pleasing events was the subscription of the King of France for six copies of his *Birds of America*. In May, 1829, he returned to America, full of delight at seeing his family again. During the next three months he hunted for birds and animals with which to enrich his collection for publication.

Returning to England accompanied by his wife, he found that he had been elected a Fellow of the Royal Society of London, a great honor, since only persons of recognized merit and talents were admitted. In 1830 Audubon began to prepare his *Ornithological Biography of the Birds of America*. This contained nearly a thousand pages, and he wrote industriously, a Mr. McGillivray of Edinburgh assisting him in preparing it for publication. In March, 1831, his book was about completed, and he speaks in his Journal of spending a few days in Liverpool and "traveling on that extraordinary road, called the railway, at the rate of twenty-four miles an hour." He also says, "I have balanced my accounts with the 'Birds of America,' and the whole business is really wonderful; forty thousand dollars have passed through my hands for the completion of the first volume. Who would believe that a lonely individual who landed in England without a friend in the whole country and with only one sovereign in his pocket [when he reached London], could extricate himself from his difficulties, not by borrowing money, but by rising at four in the morning, working hard all day, and disposing of his works at a price which a common laborer would have thought little more than sufficient remuneration for his work? . . . During the four years required to bring the first volume before the world, no less than fifty of my subscribers, representing the sum of fifty-six thousand dollars, abandoned me."

Audubon felt that he must return again to America to explore for new birds to add to his book. He went to Florida and later to Labrador, where he collected one hundred and seventy-three skins of birds and studied the habits of the eider duck, loons, wild geese, etc. Returning to London once more, in 1834 and 1835 he published the second and third volumes of his *Ornithological Biography*, going again to America in 1836 for further research. Another trip to England saw the finish of his great work. It is noteworthy evidence of the indomitable perseverance of the man that he persisted in this frequent crossing of the ocean, for the sake of his work, although he suffered great misery and discomfort from the sea voyages.

In 1839 Audubon came back to New York, purchasing a home on the banks of the Hudson, to which he gave the name of Minnie Land, in honor of his wife, Minnie being the Scotch word for mother and the name by which he usually addressed her. He had for many years desired to visit the Rocky Mountains, and in 1843 he went to the Yellowstone with a party, in order to gather material for a book on the *Quadrupeds of America*. From the results of this expedition, undertaken when he was sixty years old, three volumes were published. He himself was equal only to the preparation of the first volume, his sons completing the others after his death in January, 1851.

Of John James Audubon one writer has said:

Of the naturalists of America, no one stands out in more picturesque relief than he. He undertook and accomplished one of the most gigantic tasks that has ever fallen to the lot of man to perform. For more than three-quarters of a century his splendid paintings . . . which for spirit and vigor are still unsurpassed, have been the admiration of the world. As a field naturalist he was at his best and had few equals. He was a keen observer, and possessed the rare gift of instilling into his writings the freshness of nature and the vivacity and enthusiasm of his own personality. His was a type now rarely met, combining the grace and culture of the Frenchman, with the candor, patience and earnestness of purpose of the American.

As a pioneer in an unknown field he naturally made some mistakes, but he was always sincere and honest in presenting his convictions. Another writer said:

> He has enlarged and enriched the domains of a pleasing and useful science; he has revealed to us the existence of many species of birds before unknown; he has given us more accurate information of the forms and habits of those that were known; and he has imparted to the study of natural history the grace and fascination of romance.

The National Audubon Society is a fitting monument to this lover of birds. It sustains the Audubon wardens, the minute men of the coast, whose duty it is to protect the waterfowl from destruction because of their service to humanity as the scavengers of the coast region. It maintains havens for the birds at nesting time; and in many ways protects our feathered friends.

Louis Agassiz

"I WISH it may be said of Louis Agassiz that he was the first naturalist of his time, a good citizen, and a good son, beloved of all who knew him." Such was the expression of the life-purpose of a young man at the age of twenty-one, and in every way Jean Louis Rudolphe Agassiz attained the goal he had set before himself.

Switzerland was the land of his birth. His father was a clergyman, his mother the daughter of a physician. They were his only teachers for the first ten years of his life. His love of natural history was early evident. The pet animals he had were not only an amusement and a pleasure but also a source of information, for he was ever eager to observe their habits. From the freshwater fish in the Lake of Morat, on the shore of which was his home, he gained the beginnings of the wonderful knowledge of their characteristics which later in life so astonished the audiences to whom he lectured.

At the age of ten he was sent to the boys' school at Bienne, where nine hours of study daily, alternated with intervals for rest and play, kept him busy and happy. At fifteen, when his parents planned to have him enter commercial life he begged for two more years of study and, his request being granted, he went to the college at Lausanne. His uncle, a physician in that city, noting the boy's interest in anatomy, urged that he be allowed to study medicine, and therefore at the end of his college course Louis entered a medical school at Zurich.

Here fortune favored him, for his professor of natural history and physiology gave him the key to his private library and his collection of birds. As Louis was without financial means to purchase books, he made good use of this kindness by spending hours in copying the books he could not otherwise obtain, aided in this by his brother Auguste.

In the spring of 1826 the young student went to the University of Heidelberg. There he was specially interested in the magnificent collection of fossils belonging to Professor Bronn, the paleontologist, which, in 1859, was purchased by the Museum of Comparative Zoölogy at Cambridge, Massachusetts, and Agassiz had the satisfaction of using it in his work with American pupils.

Through a friendship formed at the University of Munich, Agassiz found the first stepping-stone to his later fame. The King of Bavaria had sent on an exploring expedition to Brazil two naturalists, Von Martius and Spix. They proposed on their return to publish a natural history of Brazil, but Spix died before the work was completed and Von Martius asked Agassiz to prepare the part relating to the fishes. The work was written in Latin and did much to establish for him a reputation for accurate and thorough research. At that time he was under twenty-two years of age.

An amusing incident of his student life is related by a friend: "Under Agassiz's new style of housekeeping the coffee is made in a machine which is devoted during the day to the soaking of all sorts of creatures for skeletons and in the evening again to the brewing of our tea."

On April 3, 1830, Louis Agassiz received the degree of doctor of medicine, having already won that of doctor of philosophy. He was told by the dean that "the faculty congratulate themselves on being able to give a diploma to a young man who has already acquired so honorable a reputation." Seventy-four theses were prepared by Louis in connection with the taking of the medical degree. At twenty-three years of age Louis Agassiz had won unusual honors, but unfortunately they did not furnish him with sufficient income. He was receiving at that time only forty dollars a month, out of which he was paying twenty-five dollars to the artist who illustrated his books. He expressed regret at not possessing a suitable coat to wear when presenting letters of introduction. At this critical moment, when he feared he should have to give up the studies, in which he was becoming famous, to teach in order to earn a living, Von Humboldt sent him a letter of credit for one thousand francs. Through the influence of this friend he obtained a professorship in natural history at Neuchâtel, where he helped to build up a museum of natural history, and to make the town a center of scientific activity.

A great trial now came to him, for his eyes, injured by the long strain of peering through the microscope, compelled him to stop work for several months and live in a darkened room. During this period he practiced the study of fossils by touch, using even the tip of his tongue to get the impression when his fingers were not sufficiently sensitive. He felt sure he could cultivate such delicacy of touch that if eyesight failed him he would not need to abandon his beloved research study. In time, to his great joy, the condition of his eyes improved. Von Humboldt wrote: "For mercy's sake, take care of your eyes; they are ours."

Recognition of his scientific ability and offers of co-operation came to him from all over the world. The Wollaston prize of one thousand pounds sterling was bestowed upon him by the Royal Society of London, of which he was later made a member. It aided him to continue production of his famous book entitled *Researches on the Fossil Fishes,* describing over seven hundred species. It took ten years to complete this work. Having learned to know accurately one thousand five hundred species of fishes, he made a new classification of the whole genus, fossils and living. But he remained an opponent of the Darwinian theory, believing that development meant development of plan as expressed in structure, not the change from one structure into another.

The science of conchology had hitherto been based almost wholly upon the study of empty shells. Considering this superficial, Agassiz adopted the method of obtaining casts from the inner molding of the shells, by which the perfect form of the animal was reproduced. This method is now universally used.

His visit to England, at the urgent invitation of leading men who offered him the use of valuable collections of fishes, brought him both honor and enjoyment. Offers of professorships at Geneva and Lausanne did not tempt him to leave Neuchâtel, and the appreciation of the citizens was expressed in a letter of thanks in which he was asked to accept a gift of six thousand francs.

In 1846 he sailed for America, the King of Prussia having given him fifteen thousand francs to pursue investigations in the ichthyology of this country. On his arrival he began a course of lectures at the Lowell Institute, on the "Plan of Creation, especially in the Animal Kingdom." His power as a teacher and his personal charm won his audiences despite his unfamil-

iarity with the English language, which frequently
compelled him to pause till he found the right word.
In 1848 political changes in Europe caused his honorable discharge from the service of the King of Prussia,
and he accepted the chair of natural history in the
Lawrence Scientific School, with a salary of one thousand five hundred dollars. From there he went, in
1851, to the medical college in Charleston, South
Carolina. In May, 1854, an invitation to the University of Zurich, Switzerland, and in 1857 one from the
Emperor of France to the chair of paleontology in the
Museum of Natural History in Paris, testified to the
desire of European men of science to win him back
from America. But he declined both offers, saying he
felt the task here would take a lifetime. Despite his
twice-repeated refusal, the Emperor bestowed upon
him, a few months later, the order of the Legion of
Honor. Von Humboldt, writing to George Ticknor
with reference to this declination, said:

> I have never believed that this illustrious man, who
> is also a man of warm heart, a noble soul, would accept
> the generous offers made to him from Paris. I knew that
> gratitude would keep him in the new country where
> he finds such an immense territory to explore and such
> liberal aid in his work.

Public interest in his work was freshly aroused by
the following incident. His friend Francis Gray left a

legacy of fifty thousand dollars for the establishment of a museum of comparative zoology at Cambridge; the University gave land for a site, and the Massachusetts Legislature granted one hundred thousand dollars for buildings, on condition that private subscriptions should supplement the grant. In addition to the $75,125 raised, Agassiz gave all his zoological collections gathered during the preceding four years. These collections were worth about ten thousand dollars. Agassiz insisted that the museum should not be named for him, although popular wish has invariably called it the Agassiz Museum.

Previous to the founding of this museum Agassiz had planned a series of volumes entitled *Contributions to the Natural History of the United States.* Subscriptions to this work far exceeded his expectations, for 2100 were secured at twelve dollars a volume before publication commenced.

An early sympathizer with women's desire for advanced study, Professor Agassiz threw his college courses open to women as well as men at about this time. In this way he helped foster feminine interest in original scientific investigation.

Agassiz believed in teaching his students, male and female, to learn by observation and comparison. Their first lesson was simply one in looking. Left with a simple specimen, Nathaniel Shaler, one of Agassiz's early students, was told to use his eyes diligently and report what he found. After a hundred hours or so spent in examining the specimen, he reported to the professor. An hour's recitation ensued, at the end of which time he was dismissed with the remark, "That is not right." After another week of ten hours' labor a day, during which the teacher never asked a leading question of the pupil, never pointed out a single feature in the specimen, never prompted an inference or a conclusion, Shaler had some satisfactory results. Moreover, he had learned something that many students never learn. He discovered that he was "capable of doing hard, continuous work without the support of a teacher." The lesson was invaluable, and it stimulated Shaler and many another young student to original research.

The Civil War began, and no American cared more than Agassiz did for the preservation of the Union and the institutions which it represents. He urged the founding of a national academy of sciences, and was active in its organization and incorporation by Congress. As an evidence of his faith in the Constitution of the United States and the justice of her cause, he formally became one of her citizens. Writing to Sir Philip Edgerton, Agassiz said: "I feel I have a debt to pay to my adopted country, and all I can now do is to contribute my share toward maintaining the scientific activity which has been awakened during the last few years."

In 1865 Agassiz planned a trip to Brazil for scientific study, and Nathaniel Thayer of Boston offered him six assistants with all expenses paid; the Pacific Mail Steamship Company invited him to take the whole party on their fine steamship, the *Colorado,* as far as Rio de Janeiro, free of charge, and the Secretary of the United States Navy desired all officers of vessels of war stationed along the coast to give him aid and support. Agassiz wrote: "I seem like the spoiled child of the country, and I hope God will give me strength to repay in devotion to her institutions and to her scientific and intellectual development, all that her citizens have done for me."

With characteristic ardor he pushed a plan of a summer school for teachers for the direct study of nature. John Anderson of New York offered him a site on the island of Penikese, in Buzzards Bay, with an endowment of fifty thousand dollars for equipment. Again Agassiz refused to have his own name given to the school and suggested that of the Anderson School of Natural History. It was opened in June, 1873. From the hundreds of applicants the zoologist selected thirty men and twenty women. Whittier's poem, "The Prayer of Agassiz," commemorates the opening.

At length the busy, enthusiastic life closed on December 14, 1873, and he was buried at Mount Auburn. The boulder that marks his grave came from a glacier of the Aar, not far from where his hut stood when he was on one of his exploring expeditions; and the pine which shelters it was sent from his old home in Switzerland. "The land of his birth and the land of his adoption are united at his grave."

Carl Schurz

"ONE whose migration to America must be put on the credit side of the immigration account." This was the comment of a leading weekly of the United States on the life of Carl Schurz, who, throughout his residence in this country, gave in all things full proof of his patriotism.

Carl, the son of a peasant schoolmaster, was born in 1829, in Liblar, a short distance from Cologne. In those days, before the emergence of Germany as a unified national state, districts sometimes changed kings over night, being ruled now by one petty prince, now by another. During the course of one of these changes, Liblar came under the control of the autocratic King of Prussia, to the dismay of the freedom-loving townspeople. There was much talk of freedom and even rebellion in the small town, particularly in the gymnasium where Carl was at school. Indeed, Carl wrote a fiery composition on the subject of liberty, so fiery, in fact, that his rather timid schoolmaster, fearing trouble with the authorities, rebuked him for his effort. Smarting under the unjust criticism, Carl held his feelings in check, awaiting a more sympathetic audience.

In 1846, upon entering the University of Bonn, he found his opportunity. These were the spirited days before the revolutions of 1848, when all of Central Europe, receiving the impulse from France, rose briefly to threaten its oppressors. In the Franconia Society, composed of students from all parts of Germany, young Carl found kindred spirits, and at the home of Professor Gottfried Kinkel, who became his friend, he found other men and women anxious to devote themselves to the cause of liberty. It was here that Carl joined a group of young revolutionaries who were ready to sacrifice themselves in order that liberty might be gained for the people. Carl was made a lieutenant in the revolutionary army that was formed. But all too soon this army was overpowered, and Carl fled for fear of being captured and shot as a rebel.

He resolved to get out of the village through a new sewer which was as yet unused. With his servant and a friend he reached the opening unnoticed and crept inside. As they were crawling through, a heavy rain suddenly filled the sewer so that only their heads were above water. At last, after many difficulties, they reached the outlet, only to find a Prussian guard on duty there. This meant that they must go back to town. There they hid in a ditch covered with brush until Carl attracted the attention of a workman, who led them to a small loft where there was just room enough for the three of them. Prussian soldiers, however, came into the shed below them, and for three nights and two days they were forced to remain there without food or drink.

At length, becoming desperate, Carl's friend managed to get down from the loft and over to a nearby hut while the soldiers were asleep. He returned with a piece of bread and an apple, and the promise of the man who lived there to bring them food, and also information as to a possible way of escape. With his aid they got away the next night, and again crawled through the sewer, which was no longer guarded. After an hour's tramp they found a boat on the bank of the Rhine, which took them across to France. Thence Schurz went to Switzerland.

After some months he heard that his friend Kinkel was in a Prussian prison, and felt that it was his duty to try to rescue him. It was a difficult and dangerous undertaking, but it was finally accomplished. The act was so daring that it created a sensation in Europe.

The next two years Schurz spent in Paris and London, where he supported himself by teaching and as correspondent for German newspapers. He then decided to go to America, and with his young bride, the daughter of a merchant of Hamburg, he reached New York in September, 1852. During the next three years he endeavored to learn all that he could about the government and laws of the United States, visiting Washington and hearing the senators and congressmen speak on the affairs of the day. He studied law, and also the conditions and needs of this country. He made public speeches to help accomplish the changes he saw were necessary. As soon as he had lived here long enough he became an American citizen. He was strongly opposed to slavery, and in 1858 he spoke in English on this subject so effectively that his speech was published all over the United States.

Schurz soon became noted as an orator, and he did a great deal to bring the Republican party into power and to elect Abraham Lincoln president of this country. He was appointed United States minister to Spain, but he did not remain there long, for the Civil War broke out and he felt he could serve his adopted country better on this side of the water. Immediately upon his return he entered the army and was made brigadier-general. Later he was promoted to the rank of major-general and took part in several dangerous engagements.

During and after the war he helped the cause of freedom by frequent public speeches. As editor of influential newspapers and as an orator, Carl Schurz aided in the election of General Grant to the presidency. In 1869 he was himself elected to the United States Senate, being the first man born in Germany to attain that honor. He held this office for six years.

He rendered great service by exposing public abuses and simultaneously imbuing the people with national ideals of a high order. Reforming the corrupt civil service was one of his outstanding contributions to his new country. He also aided in destroying the bossism of the political machine, and always strove to inspire others with his own principle of country above party, bettering Stephen Decatur's axiom by his own: "My country, right or wrong. If right, to be kept right; if wrong, to be put right."

As Secretary of the Interior under President Hayes, he helped to better the condition of the Indians and to bring them into closer touch with civilization. It has been well said that "no one could question the unselfishness of his devotion to his adopted country, the non-partisan temper of his critical judgments, and the nobility of his political ideals." Surely it would be difficult to win higher praise.

Carl Schurz was distinguished as a linguist, amazing his brother senators on one occasion by translating at sight lengthy passages on a technical subject into four different languages. "He was the only statesman of his generation who could make an eloquent speech either in English or German without revealing which was his native tongue."

Toward the end of his life, at the request of his children, Carl Schurz wrote the story of his experiences. These are entitled *Reminiscences*, and fill three large volumes, containing many interesting incidents, for which there is no space here. He died in 1906.

The tribute given him by William Dean Howells we quote in part:

> Schurz's character had the simplicity which mates with true greatness. His was a tender, affectionate nature, though never a weak one. You knew where to find him always, and that was the right place. This fighter for freedom in two worlds, this just advocate, this honest politician, this conscientious journalist, this wise statesman lived with all the honor that a man could wish.

Andrew Carnegie

IN June, 1889, there appeared in the *North American Review* an article called "The Gospel of Wealth." It bore the name of Andrew Carnegie and exalted, as conditions imposed by nature, "the concentration of business, industrial and commercial, in the hands of the few, and the law of competition between these, as being not only beneficial, but essential to the progress of the race." Perhaps there was nothing strange in finding such sentiments expressed by a man whose industrial empire, which was soon to be recapitalized at 320 million dollars, was then reaping profits of 2 million a year, especially since the author had begun life as a bobbin boy in a cotton factory at $1.20 a week. But it is curious to find that this defender of inequality, who praised the virtues to be acquired through struggle, owes his reputation to philanthropy rather than pugnacity, to charity rather than industry. And the life of Andrew Carnegie is full of such curious paradoxes: a poor boy, he became fabulously wealthy; unscrupulous in business, he donated millions to philanthropic ends; a robber baron,

he hated war; uneducated, he endowed seats of learning and introduced millions of people to cultural
influences; a rugged individualist, he prepared the
way for industry-strangling monoply; a professed
democrat, he helped to undermine democracy by con-
centrating power in the hands of a few.

The career of this paradoxical individual began on
November 25, 1835, in the small Scottish town of
Dunfermline, the town from which the king in the
old ballad sends his summons to Sir Patrick Spens. The
boy's father was a master weaver, the last of a long
succession of skilled hand weavers of damask, who
was ruined by the introduction of the power loom and
the advent of the factory system. But in the faraway
city of Pittsburgh, Pennsylvania, at the juncture of
the Allegheny and Monongahela rivers, there were
relatives, and to that industrial American city the
family turned. They settled in nearby Allegheny City
in 1847, and in a local cotton factory both William
Carnegie and his thirteen-year-old son Andrew found
work. Andrew began as a bobbin boy, soon shifting
jobs to become an engineer's assistant. The resounding
title cloaked a menial task, for he merely stoked a
steam boiler. But he was given an eighty-cent increase
in pay. Working twelve hours a day, he was now earning two dollars a week.

One evening in 1850 when Andrew returned from
work his uncle told him that a messenger boy was

wanted in the Pittsburgh telegraph office. Andrew applied for the job and, despite his smallness and his imperfect knowledge of the city, he was employed. Leaving the steam boiler and the grimy cellar, he was, he says, "lifted into paradise, yes, heaven, as it seemed to me, with newspapers, pens, pencils, and sunshine about me." Moreover, he now earned two dollars and fifty cents a week.

It was while working as a messenger boy that Carnegie made his first attempt at financial organization. The boys who delivered messages were allowed to collect an extra charge of ten cents for delivery beyond a certain area. These "dime messages" were the cause of trouble among the boys, since frequent quarrels arose over the right of delivery. Young Carnegie suggested "pooling" the messages and dividing the extra money equally among the boys. His suggestion was adopted, and he was made treasurer of the pool. Thereafter, as he tells it, "Peace and good humor reigned."

Despite Andrew's solution of the problem, he was not popular with the other messenger boys. He was accused of being penurious, never spending his share of extra dimes for candy and buns as the other boys did. Moreover, he lectured the others on their extravagance. But his close ways and good manners were well thought of by the manager, who often chose Andrew to watch the office during his own absence. This extra work won him a slight raise in pay. It also provided him with an opportunity to learn telegraphy, an opportunity which he put to unexpected use one morning when an urgent message came through before the regular operator arrived for duty. Taking the message accurately, Andrew was rewarded for his diligence by being assigned as a substitute operator during another emergency. Before long he was made a regular operator at a salary of twenty-five dollars a month.

Though young Andrew had been working hard, he had not spent all of his time in the telegraph office. Through the kindness of Colonel James Anderson, who had opened his private library to Pittsburgh working boys, Carnegie was able to borrow a book a week. In later years he attributed his own benefactions in founding libraries to the example of Colonel Anderson. To the same man, who had often helped him in his selection of books, he owed his appreciation of literature, a taste which, he asserted, he "would not exchange for all the millions that were ever amassed by man." This taste proved even financially profitable to the young telegrapher, however. Reading history gave him an interest in world affairs, and he was able to earn an extra dollar a week making copies of the foreign news reports that came over his wire and distributing them to local newspapers.

Carnegie next sought to ingratiate himself with Thomas A. Scott, divisional superintendent of the Pennsylvania Railroad at Pittsburgh and, purportedly, "one of the shrewdest intriguers in the railroad business." Offered a job as railroad telegrapher and secretary to Scott, Andrew immediately accepted. Shortly thereafter an accident occurred on one of the lines during Scott's absence. Andrew took it upon himself to order the resumption of schedules—an order that only Scott could give—in his boss's name. The order saved time for the line, but it might have cost lives. Since the episode had no serious consequences, the wily superintendent kept his "white-haired Scotch devil" with him, knowing that such unscrupulousness might prove useful. And so it did, for Carnegie later employed labor spies to compile a blacklist and break a strike for his boss.

At the age of sixteen Carnegie was given a stock-market tip by Scott. Mortgaging his now-widowed mother's home, he raised five hundred dollars for his first market speculation, and it proved to be successful. Some time later he met Thomas T. Woodruff, inventor of the first sleeping car, and through his connection with Scott, he was able to advance Woodruff's plan for the manufacture of the car. Carnegie borrowed enough money to invest $217.50 in the new sleeping car company, and in two years he was making $5,000 a year from this investment alone. Other investments followed, notably a "flyer" in some oil acreage which netted him many thousands of dollars. The young man was so delighted upon fruition of the latter scheme that he exclaimed, "Oh, I'm rich! I'm rich!"

The beginning of the Civil War found Carnegie, a professed Abolitionist, still working for Scott, who had become Assistant Secretary of War in charge of the Transportation Department, in Washington. But with the Union defeat at Bull Run and the prospect of a long war, both Scott and Carnegie left Washington. As a matter of fact, with the war increasing in severity, twenty-seven-year-old Andrew decided that he needed a vacation in Scotland. He left for Dunfermline on June 28, 1862, shortly after the costly battle of Shiloh had taken place. His stay in Scotland was prolonged by a siege of illness, but he returned to America before the end of the War and made plans for a career in industry, which was then beginning to flourish.

The significant work of Andrew Carnegie, like that of the carpetbaggers, was undertaken during the period of reconstruction. Through his connection with the railroads, he was able to see the importance of iron in industrial America. Shrewdly, he decided to abandon his other interests at the close of the Civil War and concentrate on iron. Within a few years he had organized or bought into companies that made iron bridges, rails, and locomotives. Then he moved to New York, the center of high finance, to act as salesman for his companies and as broker for numerous railroad and iron interests. His brashness had not deserted him with the acquisition of wealth, nor had he lost his ability to ingratiate himself with influential people. Soon he was making enormous commissions on various brokerage "deals" and plowing his winnings back into his iron interests.

In 1867, at the age of thirty-two, with an income of $50,000 a year, Carnegie decided that he wanted to quit business life. His ambition was to "settle in Oxford and get a thorough education, making the acquaintance of literary men." He made the following entry in his diary at this time:

> Man must have an idol—the amassing of money is one of the worst species of idolatry—no idol more debasing than the worship of money. . . . To continue much longer overwhelmed by business cares and with most of my thoughts wholly upon the way to make more money in the shortest time, must degrade me beyond hope of permanent recovery.

However, upon visiting London the young entrepreneur met the "crazy Frenchman" Bessemer, then working upon further experiments in steel. He saw the Bessemer converter in action and experienced a change of heart that resembled a religious conversion. "Jumping on the first available steamer, he rushed home" to Pittsburgh, shouting: "The day of Iron has passed—Steel is King!" A literary life at Oxford and hopes of permanent recovery from commercialism were forgotten, and Carnegie was on his way to amassing new fortunes in steel.

Carnegie's sudden vision of the new day of steel had been rather late in coming. Practical steel making had been under way in England for more than a decade before he realized its importance. In America, too, the brilliant Alexander Holley had been setting up Bessemer plants since 1865. Even Carnegie's own partner, William Coleman, had for over six years been urging him to go into steel manufacturing.

Despite his late start, however, Carnegie was soon turning out more Bessemer steel than all the other American mills combined. Enjoying a high protective duty which eliminated British competition, being favorably located for production, and already dominating the iron industry, Carnegie determined to supply steel to the expanding country in enormous quantities. The plant which he built in 1875, on Braddock's battlefield on the banks of the Monongahela was the largest and most elaborate steel plant in the country. A capital investment of over a million dollars made competition prohibitively costly and restricted it to a limited number of firms. And Carnegie was quick to take advantage of hard times by buying up or ruining his rivals. Underselling opponents until he had forced them out of business and then raising his prices again, he soon became known as the "pirate" of the steel industry.

Carnegie was as thoroughly hated and feared by his own working force as by rival industrialists whom he had ruined. His labor policy was, in the words of a historian of the period, "thoroughly bad." By a system of "unfriendly competition" for which he became infamous in the industry, he forced his managers and supervisors to get maximum production from his laborers for very little pay. Unionism was inhibited. The "lockout" was frequently employed in disputes. Accidents were common, for few safety precautions were taken. One of his most valuable technical aides, Captain "Billy" Jones, a man whose industrial know-how amounted to genius, met a horrible death in an explosion of molten metal in one of the plants. This was a serious blow to Carnegie, for he himself had but the scantiest knowledge of the techniques of steel production and he had to depend upon his skilled assistants. But even these underlings were as shabbily treated as his workers. Whenever he was informed (in Pittsburgh, New York, Scotland, or wherever his scattered interests took him) of a production peak in one of his plants, Carnegie would telegraph: "Congratulations! Why not do it every week?" Or, told that one of his furnaces had broken all records, he would ask: "What were the other ten furnaces doing?"

Though Carnegie soon succeeded in dominating the steel industry through these methods, he still feared three giant antagonists. The first of these with whom he came to grips was Henry Clay Frick, who, with a monopoly of coal lands, controlled the production of coke. Carnegie knew that he "could not get on without a supply of the fuel essential to the smelting of pig iron" and, rather than risk a war with the millionaire baron of coke, he joined forces with him. In 1889 Frick became general manager, under Carnegie, of the tremendous combine formed from the two industries.

John D. Rockefeller, privately referred to as "Reck a fellow" by Carnegie, was another thorn in the Scotsman's side. He had acquired, in addition to his oil lands, large sections of the Mesabi Range, the richest ore lands in the world. Carnegie feared a "squeeze" on another essential raw material, and he hastily bought some acreage in the Range to use as a bargaining lever. Then he began to bargain with "my dear fellow millionaire," as he addressed his rival directly. When negotiations were completed Carnegie held, by lease or ownership, two thirds of the Mesabi deposits. The Carnegie companies also "owned and controlled mines producing 6,000,000 tons of ore annually; 40,000 acres of coal land and 12,000 coke ovens; steamship lines for transporting ore to Lake Erie ports; docks for handling ore and coal and a railroad from Lake Erie to Pittsburgh; 70,000 acres of natural gas territory with 200 miles of pipe line; nineteen blast furnaces and five steel mills producing and finishing 3,250,000 tons of steel annually."

But, even when entrenched behind the massive vertical wall of his combine, Carnegie was still vulnerable. J. P. Morgan, the banker, was busily amalgamating metal trusts and railroads in a network of interlocking directorates that would eventually be capable of undermining any company, no matter how large. Carnegie began to feel the pinch when the Pennsylvania Railroad suddenly doubled his freight rates. He determined to fight, and he was ready to use the millions he held in reserve to build a new railroad and cut his way to the sea. Then he would undertake a steel war in earnest, wrecking his opponents and himself, if necessary. The master banker, Morgan, saw his cunningly fabricated empire tottering and he decided to stop the war by buying Carnegie out. In 1901 Carnegie sold his companies to J. P. Morgan for $492,000,000. The price, according to Morgan, "made Carnegie the richest man in the world." It also made U. S. Steel, the corporation Morgan formed with his new holdings, the largest and most powerful monoply in America.

No longer concerned with "the way to make more money in the shortest possible time," the richest man in the world now sought to perpetuate his memory through the distribution of some of his uncountable millions of dollars. His first charitable act was to establish a fund to be used in caring for aged employees who had worn out their lives in his service. Then, having derived all the education he had from reading, he sought to make books available to greater numbers of people, contributing close to $60,000,000 to public libraries. He endowed the Carnegie Institute of Washington, D.C., with $25,000,000 "to encourage . . . research and discovery, and the application of knowledge to the improvement of mankind." In Pittsburgh, where he had made his fortune, Carnegie spent $28,-000,000 on an institute which embraced a library, a museum, a picture gallery, and the Carnegie School of Technology. The Carnegie Corporation of New York received $125,000,000 for the advancement of education and research. Such widely separated and diverse institutions as the Mount Wilson Observatory in California and the University of St. Andrews in Scotland benefited by his gifts. And he donated money for a variety of causes ranging from a pension fund for aged university professors to contributions for church organs. In all he distributed something over $350,-000,000.

Of course, Andrew Carnegie deserves praise for his gifts. Though people who knew him asserted that he "never gave anything without the requirement that his name be attached to the gift," the men and women who have read in the libraries, studied in the schools, or worked in the laboratories that Carnegie endowed have profited no less fully. Nevertheless, our praise for the bringer of such gifts must be qualified by our knowledge of the man and of the spirit in which he gave. And the paradoxical Carnegie seems to have given millions from a variety of contradictory reasons. Gratitude, patriotism, love for humanity doubtless influenced him in some degree. But in an age when Rockefeller, Morgan, Mellon, and Frick were distributing millions to sweeten their unsavory reputations and enshrine their memories, philanthropy was a competitive business which Andrew Carnegie could hardly resist. Since his own reputation needed some sweetening, his gifts were bound to be large. It has been pointed out, moreover, that "the distribution of immense charities, no less than sumptuary extravagance" is a form of "conspicuous consumption" designed to call attention to "successful predatory aggression." And few were more successful in this sphere than Andrew Carnegie.

Carnegie died in 1919. He is remembered, as he wished to be, through the numerous charities which he established. His role as a baron of steel is almost forgotten now, concealed behind the mask of the philanthropist which he donned in his later years. Perhaps this is the greatest paradox of his contradictory career. As Eugene Schneider, head of the Creusot Steel Works in France, said of him after his death: "He gave the little recognized contribution to the progress of the world, namely, that he popularized steel, and showed that cheap steel is one of the greatest gifts ever produced for mankind."

John Muir

IN 1838, among the wilds of Scotland, at Dunbar by the stormy North Sea, a boy was born who was always to delight in nature and who even in his old age would climb almost inaccessible mountains and travel long journeys into unfrequented places. John Muir was the eldest son of hard-working Scotch people and had few pleasures. He was sent to school when only three years old, his grandfather having previously taught him the letters of the alphabet from the street signs opposite his home.

School was not a place of enjoyment for John, for, like many another boy, he was mischievous and venturesome and paid the penalty by having frequent thrashings. Between the age of seven and eight he left the "Auld Davel Brae Schule" for the grammar school. Here he had three lessons a day in Latin, three in French, and as many in English, in addition to spelling, arithmetic, history, and geography. At home his father made him learn so many verses of the Bible that when he was eleven years old he knew by heart three quarters of the Old Testament and all of the New

Testament. As he himself quaintly puts it: "By sore flesh I was able to recite the New Testament from the beginning to the end without a single stop, for the grand, simple, all-sufficient Scotch discovery had been made that there was a close connection between the skin and the memory, and that irritation of the skin excited the memory to any required degree."

Boys of today would surely think themselves badly treated if they were given the meals John Muir and his brothers and sisters had. For breakfast they had oatmeal porridge with a little milk or molasses. Dinner consisted usually of vegetable broth, a small piece of boiled mutton, and barley scone. For tea they were given half a slice of white bread without butter, barley scone, and a drink called "content," which was simply warm water with a little milk and sugar. For supper they had a boiled potato and barley scone. The only fire for the whole house was in the little kitchen stove, the firebox of which was eight inches long and eight inches in width and depth.

Into the monotony of this life came one day a joyous surprise when Father Muir said, "Bairns, you needna learn your lessons the nicht, for we're gaen to America the morn." For many years after that John's home was at Kingston, near Fort Winnebago, Wisconsin. The heavy burden of clearing and plowing the land fell on him, although he was only twelve years old. One of his particularly hard experiences was the digging of the well, into which he was lowered every morning at sunrise, and there spent the day chiseling away the hard rock, except for a short interval at noon. This slow method occupied many months and was a great trial to a boy who loved outdoor life. When he had reached a depth of eighty feet he nearly lost his life by being overcome with gas. In that pioneer existence there was much hardship. At one time when he was sick with the mumps he was kept at work in the harvest field even though he fainted more than once. For several weeks he was ill with pneumonia, but he had to struggle through without any aid from a doctor.

At fifteen years of age John Muir became eager for an education. He borrowed such books as he could get and, because his father would not let him stay up at night, he rose at one o'clock every morning, studying in the cellar as the warmest place in the cold winter days. He developed a talent for invention, making his own tools out of the materials at hand. He made a fine saw out of strips of steel from old corsets; bradawls, punches, and a pair of compasses from wire and old files. He constructed a timekeeper which indicated the days of the month and of the week as well as the hours. One of his clocks kept good time for fifty years. He also built a self-setting sawmill and an automatic contrivance for feeding horses at a required hour.

Soon after Muir became of age he left home, with

only fifteen dollars in his pocket, with which to make his way in the world. He went to the State Fair and exhibited his inventions, which elicited much wonder and interest. At the age of twenty-two he entered the University of Wisconsin, discovering that, although he had not attended school since he left Scotland except for two months in a district school, a few weeks in the preparatory department enabled him to qualify as a freshman. He spent four years at the university. In his book, *My Boyhood and Youth,* he says: "I earned enough during summer vacations to pay thirty-two dollars a year for instruction, my books, acids, retorts, glass tubes, etc. I had to cut down expenses for board to half a dollar a week."

During this period he invented an apparatus which, when attached to his bed, not only awakened him at a definite hour but simultaneously lighted a lamp. After so many minutes allotted for dressing, a book was pushed up from a rack below the top of his desk, thrown open, and allowed to remain there a certain number of minutes. Then the machinery closed the book, dropped it back into its place, and moved the rack forward with the next book required.

Having completed his work at the university, John Muir started on a trip to Canada on foot. He worked in a mill there for a year, improving its machinery and inventing appliances for increasing its product. Then he went to Indianapolis and in a carriage and wagon factory was offered the position of foreman with a prospective partnership. But through an accident one of his eyes was injured, and after several weeks of confinement in a dark room he decided "to get away into the flowery wilderness to enjoy and lay in a large stock of God's wild beauty before the coming on of the time of darkness." He therefore went on foot on a botanizing tour to Cedar Keys on the Gulf of Mexico, and later he traveled to Cuba. In 1868 he went to California. There in the Yosemite he lived for many years, occasionally taking trips to still wilder places. He climbed the most inaccessible mountains and discovered some sixty-five glaciers. One of his remarkable feats was crawling along a three-inch ledge to the brink of the 1600-foot plunge of the Upper Yosemite creek to listen, as he said, "to the sublime psalm of the falls."

In 1879 he went to Alaska and, while there, he had an adventure which revealed the indomitable character of the man. Mr. Muir and his friend, S. Hall Young, were together on a mountain-climbing expedition. Mr. Young's book, *Alaska Days with John Muir*, tells us:

> Then Muir began to slide up that mountain. A deer-lope over the smoother slopes, a sure instinct for the easiest way into a rocky fortress, an instant and unerring attack, a serpent glide up the steep; eye, hand, and foot all dynamically connected, with no appear-

ance of weight to his body. . . . Fifteen years of enthusiastic study in the Sierras had given him preëminence over the ordinary climber. . . . No Swiss guide was ever wiser in the habits of glaciers than Muir. . . . Not an instant when both feet and hands were not in play; often elbows, knees, thighs, upper arms, and even chin must grip and hold. Clambering up a steep slope, crawling under an overhanging rock, spreading out like a flying squirrel, and edging along an inch-wide projection while fingers clasped knobs above the head, bending about sharp angles, pulling up smooth rock faces by sheer strength of arm, and chinning over the edge, leaping fissures, sliding flat around a dangerous rock breast, testing crumbling spurs before risking his weight, always going up, up, no hesitation, no pause—that was Muir.

While climbing Mr. Young met with an accident which deprived him of the use of his arms, both shoulders being dislocated. In this dilemma he was practically helpless, but Mr. Muir was equal to the occasion and in a marvelous way climbed over glaciers and down the steepest crags, supporting his friend. It took all night to do it, but he succeeded. The story is a thrilling one. It concludes thus:

Sometimes he would pack me for a short distance on his back. Again taking me by the wrist he would swing me down to a lower level before descending himself. Holding my collar by his teeth as a panther her cub, and clinging like a squirrel to a tree, he climbed with me straight up ten or twelve feet, with only the help of my ironshod feet scrambling on the rock. All night this man of steel and lightning worked, never resting a minute, doing the work of three men, always cheery, full of joke and anecdote, inspiring me with his own indomitable spirit. He gave heart to me.

In one of his climbing expeditions Muir suddenly found the ground under him slipping. Instantly he threw himself on his back, spread out both arms, and so took a ride on an avalanche.

But though Muir was so great a traveler, going in 1903 and 1914 to Europe, the Caucasus, Siberia, Japan, China, India, Egypt, Australia, and New Zealand for botanical study, and even at the age of seventy-three making a trip to the wilderness on the Amazon River and then to the jungles of Africa, it is to his love for and investigations in the Yosemite that we are indebted for our possession as a nation of the most noted and wonderful of our national parks. Largely because of his earnest and persistent efforts the Yosemite was made a national reserve in 1890. It is thirty-six miles in length and forty-eight in breadth. The Yosemite Valley lies in the heart of it. It includes two rivers, innumerable lakes and waterfalls, forests, ice-sculptured cañons, and mountains twelve thousand feet high. In his book, *The Yosemite*, the wonders and beauty of this marvelous region are fully described by this man who had given years of study to it. Other works by him are *Mountains of California*,

Our National Parks, My First Summer in the Sierra,
and many magazine articles. His story, *Stickeen,*
about a favorite dog in Alaska, ranks with *Rab and
His Friends,* and *Bob, Son of Battle.* In each of his
writings one glimpses the far-reaching knowledge of
nature and animal life that he had acquired.

In the spring of 1880 Mr. Muir married Miss Louise
Strentzel, daughter of a Polish physician who had arrived in California in 1847. Muir had a happy home,
but much as he loved it and his friends, he loved nature more ardently. His devotion to it was the master
passion of his life, and he himself recognized that he
was "hopelessly and forever a mountaineer." "Few
have loved beauty as I have, enough to forego so much
to attain it." His home was a ranch forty miles from
San Francisco. As soon as his vineyard was ready for
the summer he would go to his loved mountains,
where for three months he enjoyed every moment,
living mainly on bread and tea. He fairly reveled in
an earthquake that he might see the changes wrought
by such a convulsion of nature. He would climb to the
top of swaying branches to feel the pulsing of the
heart of a storm. After these experiences he was wont
to say, "We have met with God." Tyndall said Muir
was the greatest authority on glacial action the world
has known, and Agassiz and Le Conte held a similar
opinion. To the largest glacier (one in Alaska) Muir's
name has been given. When he discovered it, it was

fully a mile and a half in width and the perpendicular face of it towered from four to seven hundred feet above the water.

A writer in the *Craftsman* has well said:

Muir was Scotch to the backbone, yet America claims him as her own, so earnestly has he studied our trees, so closely is he identified with the wonders of the great West, so loyally has he labored to preserve our natural beauties when from time to time there have been those of our countrymen who would have wrested them from us. A mighty Alaskan glacier bears his name, a noble forest of California redwoods —Muir Woods—and it is likewise fitting that a little mountain daisy is his namesake, [for he would speak of a tiny fern as] one of the bonnies of our Father's bairns.

Alexander Graham Bell

"IT talks!" exclaimed Dom Pedro, Emperor of Brazil, when at the Centennial Exposition in Philadelphia in 1876 he took up a telephone receiver and put it to his ear. Then Lord Kelvin, electrical scientist of the first rank and engineer of the Atlantic cable, took his turn at the strange new instrument. "It does speak," he said. "It is the most wonderful thing I have seen in America." And so one after another notable man listened and was astonished. Thus the telephone made its first public appearance. It was the most dramatic event of the exposition which displayed many remarkable inventions.

The man who had invented this marvelous instrument was Alexander Graham Bell, who was born in Edinburgh, Scotland, on March 1, 1847. He was educated at the Royal High School of his native city and in London. But his relatives had the largest share in preparing him for his success in life. Grandfather, uncle, father, and two brothers had all specialized in the study of the laws of speech and sound and had taught and written on that subject, so that through them he secured knowledge which was of great help to him in his discovery of the principle of the telephone. In London, soon after he reached the age of twenty-one and while he was teaching elocution, experiments in producing vibrations on tuning-forks by means of an electromagnet aroused in him an enthusiasm for scientific discovery.

But his progress was hindered by illness. Tuberculosis caused the death of two brothers, and he himself was threatened with the same dread disease. In hope of averting the danger, he and his father and mother left Scotland for Canada, where at Brantford he fortunately succeeded in overcoming the trouble, meanwhile interesting himself in teaching a tribe of Mohawk Indians a sign language invented by his father and called "Visible Speech," each letter representing a certain action of the lips and tongue. He had previously, in London, been particularly successful in using it to teach deaf-mutes to talk. He was offered five hundred dollars by the Board of Education of Boston to introduce the system in a school for deaf-mutes. Alexander Bell gladly accepted, and his teaching met with such success that he won a professorship in Boston University and also started a school of vocal physiology which proved profitable.

These occupations interfered with the pursuance of his inventive ideas, but at the end of two years he found opportunity to carry on his experiments in the

home of a deaf-mute pupil in Salem. The father of
the boy, Thomas Sanders, became deeply interested
and eventually was closely associated with the development of Bell's great invention, paying practically
all expenses until success was attained. Gardiner G.
Hubbard, the father of another deaf-mute pupil, was
a well-known Boston lawyer, and he too co-operated
in carrying out Bell's plans. His daughter Mabel became the wife of the young inventor four years later,
and was very helpful to him. But for the assistance of
these two men it may have been impossible for Bell to
succeed, for he had given up his professorship and his
school in order to use his time for experiments. He was
convinced that it would be possible to construct an
instrument that would actually convey the sound of
the human voice, and patiently he toiled by day and
by night to find the principle on which it could be
done.

At the suggestion of Dr. Clarence Blake, he experimented with a real ear cut from the head of a dead
man. From that he conceived the idea of a telephone
formed of two discs, like ear-drums, far apart and
connected by an electrified wire to catch the vibrations of sound at one end and reproduce them at the
other. It was on an afternoon in June, 1875, that Bell
caught the first faint sound over the wire, but more
patient study and effort had to be made before words
were audible. At last, on March 10, 1876, to the almost wild delight of Bell and his assistant, Thomas

Watson, the words, "Watson, come here, I want you," spoken by Bell in a room up three flights of stairs, at 109 Court Street, Boston, were heard distinctly by Watson in the basement. On his twenty-ninth birthday (March 1, 1876) Bell received the patent securing his rights as inventor of the telephone.

With the exception of the few scientific men who heard it at the Centennial Exposition, no one put any faith in what Lord Kelvin described as "the greatest marvel yet achieved by the electric telegraph." Men of business said, "It is only a scientific toy; it can never be a practical necessity." It seemed so absurd to speak into a tube or box that Bell was ridiculed as "a crank who says he can talk through a wire." Yet so confident was the young inventor of the ultimate results of his discovery, that in a public address at Kensington, England, in 1878, he said:

It is conceivable that cables of telephone wires could be laid underground or suspended overhead, connecting up by branch wires private dwellings, country houses, shops, manufacturing establishments, etc., and also connecting cities and towns and various places throughout the country. I am aware that such ideas may appear to you utopian and out of place, but I believe that such a scheme will be the ultimate result of the introduction of the telephone to the public.

His faith has been abundantly justified.

The Bell telephone as first exhibited was simply an old cigar-box and two hundred feet of wire, with a magnet from a toy fishpond, but it demonstrated the possibility of making the human voice audible to a person at a distance and out of sight. On October 9, 1876, the first conversation between two places was conducted over a wire two miles long, from Boston to Cambridge, Massachusetts. The actual words spoken and heard were published in the *Boston Advertiser* of October 19, and a little later the *Boston Globe* reported a lecture delivered in Salem and transmitted by telephone over a space of sixteen miles. In 1880 there was speech over a wire forty miles long, from Boston to Providence; and in 1885 a long-distance line was built from New York to Philadelphia; and in 1893 one from New York to Chicago In 1896 the Rocky Mountain Bell Company had erected a seventy-thousand-mile system for the far West.

But before all this happened many disappointments and discouraging experiences had come to the men who had so persistently believed in and worked for the great discovery. For a long time it was almost impossible to persuade business men that the telephone could be of practical use to them. Then the Western Union Telegraph Company realized that it had a competitor and proceeded to fight it with all the means at its command. It induced Thomas Edison, Amos Dolbear, and Elisha Gray to invent an instrument which it advertised as the only original telephone. This action stimulated interest, and capitalists began to take hold of Bell's patents, organizing a company to develop the business in New England. Mr. Theodore Vail was made general manager, and he started to create a national telephone system. For seventeen months after Bell's invention was known no one disputed his claim, but as its value began to be appreciated other claimants appeared, and the Bell company had to engage in a patent war that continued for eleven years and included six hundred lawsuits. At last, in 1879, the Western Union acknowledged it could not prove its case, admitted that Bell was the original inventor of the telephone and that his patents were valid.

"Every telephone in the world is still made on the plan that Bell discovered. In the actual making of it there was no one with Bell or before him. He invented it first and alone." Others have made it more perfect and useful, until today "a telephone on a desk, instead of being the simple device first in use, contains no less than one hundred and thirty pieces, with a salt-spoonful of glistening granules of carbon."

After years of struggle and hardship, success came rapidly. Bell and the men who had helped him during those years of poverty, one after the other, sold out their interests in the telephone company and became millionaires. Mr. Bell himself refused an offer of ten thousand dollars a year to be the chief inventor of the company, saying he "could not invent to order." He had a handsome house in Washington and a summer home of seven hundred acres at Cape Breton, Nova Scotia, where he devoted his time to researches for the benefit of the human race. He invented the photophone and the induction balance. Men on battlefields and in hospitals have been grateful to him for his invention of the telephone-probe for the painless detection of bullets in the human body. For this he was given the honorary degree of M.D. by the University of Heidelberg. The Emperor of Japan bestowed on him the highest order in his gift—that of the Rising Sun. The Royal Society of Great Britain and the Society of Fine Arts of London gave him medals. The Government of France made him an officer of the Legion of Honor and awarded him the Volta prize of fifty thousand francs. He devoted this gift to the establishment and endowment of the Volta Bureau in Washington, for the "increase and diffusion of knowledge relating to the deaf." He also founded the American Association to Promote the Teaching of Speech to the Deaf, to which he contributed two hundred and fifty thousand dollars.

Rarely does any man within his own lifetime see such an extensive and wonderful development of the product of his own brain and hand as Alexander Graham Bell witnessed before he died in 1922. It is one of the marvels of our age. It is really a fascinating story and is well told by Herbert Casson in his book,

The History of the Telephone. In brief, it is this: The Bell telephone secured its first million dollars of capital in 1879; its first million dollars of earning in 1882; its first million dollars of dividends in 1884; its first million dollars of surplus in 1885. It began to send a million messages a day in 1888; strung its first million miles of wire by 1900, and installed its first million telephones by 1898. At the end of 1921 there were 13,380,000 Bell stations in the United States, with a total of twelve billion calls for that year.

In 1927, only five years after Bell's death, the first transoceanic telephone conversation took place, between New York and London. And on April 25, 1935, Walter S. Gifford of the Bell System talked to Theodore Miller, in the next room, on a round-the-world phone circuit stretching from New York to London, Amsterdam, Bandoeng (Java), San Francisco, and back to New York. Telephoning, meanwhile, was fast becoming a universal practice. By 1951, the seventy-fifth anniversary of the invention of the telephone, there were nearly 75 million phones in service throughout the world. Of that number, close to 50 million, or 28 phones for every 100 persons, were in the United States, and they were being used at the rate of 200 million calls per day.

Big and little business are alike dependent upon the telephone for the conduct of their affairs. Rural dwellers have had phones installed and find ready access through them to the communities upon which they rely. The importance of the telephone in government is illustrated by the fact that Washington, D.C., has the highest phone saturation of any city in the world —over seventy phones for every hundred persons. In times of fire, flood, and danger of any kind the telephone is instantly called into use. In war it is of invaluable service. The wireless telephone has already proved a marvelous asset to the transportation industry, hundreds of thousands of mobile units having been installed in buses, trucks, and taxis, airplanes, trains, cars, and boats of all kinds. With the development of ultrashort-range radio frequencies for wireless phones, a greater general use of mobile telephones can be anticipated. Research is also being conducted on an instrument that will not only transmit, but also record and reproduce messages received in the subscriber's absence. The potentialities of Bell's invention have by no means been exhausted.

At the National Geographic Society dinner in Washington, D.C., on March 7, 1916, U. N. Bethell, senior vice president of the American Telephone Company, proposed a toast to "the foremost figure in the creation of this American art, that distinguished American, Dr. Alexander Graham Bell, of Scotland. We all know, though, that Doctor Bell is an American as much as any Pilgrim Father ever was. Americans of his type, who could not control the accident of birth, have helped to transform a wilderness into sovereign states, and to create great industries, important cities, vast empires, and all that sort of thing. They are proud of America and America is proud of them."

Of the wonders of the modern world the telephone takes almost the first place, and its inventor will always be recognized as one of the greatest benefactors of mankind. Dr. Bell died in 1922, full of years and honors.

Joseph Pulitzer

A MAN of remarkable characteristics, a very dynamo of mental and physical force, was developed
from a young immigrant lad, aged seventeen, who
landed in Boston in 1864. He was born in Mako, Hungary, the son of an Irish mother and a Jewish father.
Upon the death of his father, Joseph decided not to be
a burden to his mother and therefore attempted to enter the army. He was rejected, however, because of a
defect in one eye. Still cherishing the idea of a military
life and hearing of the war with Mexico, he started for
the United States. He was practically penniless when
he arrived in Boston, and he could speak only a few
words of English.

Meeting a fellow countryman who had just enlisted
in a German cavalry regiment being raised in New
York city to take part in the Civil War, he determined to do likewise, and as men were much needed
he was enrolled and served until the end of the conflict.

Joseph, full of fire and energy, was always ready to
take the part of the weak and helpless. One day he

could not endure seeing the brutal treatment of a fellow soldier and, without regard to army discipline, he dared to knock down the officer who was inflicting it. Of course this action involved him in trouble, and he was arrested and imprisoned to await court-martial. Meanwhile, an old general who was very fond of a good game of chess heard that this young Hungarian was a clever player. He sent for him and many hours were passed in chess-playing, during which the general became interested in the young man, quickly discovering that he had a bright mind. Fortunately for Joseph, his new friend obtained his release.

After the army was demobilized, the immigrant lad had several hard experiences. One night, having no other place in which to sleep, he chose to stay in the public park, not knowing this was not permitted. When the policeman ordered him to move on he did so, until he came to French's Hotel, in Park Row. Learning of his plight, a man in charge of the furnace told him he might sleep in the furnace-room. Before the night was over, however, he was again sent on his way by another man who later came on duty. This curious episode has the flavor of a fairy tale, for in after years Joseph Pulitzer became owner of that very building.

Soon after this adventure he decided to go West. What little money he had took him as far as East St. Louis, Illinois. He desired to cross the Mississippi but could not pay the ferryboat fare, so he offered to serve as fireman on the ferry and pleased the captain so well that he continued to work at that task until he later secured a place as stevedore on the St. Louis wharves. He filled various positions but he was frequently handicapped by his defective eyesight.

A dangerous and hard task was given him by a St. Louis man. The charter of the St. Louis & San Francisco Railroad had to be recorded in every county of the state, and the papers in the case had to be filed with the clerk of each county. As Missouri was at this time infested with bushwhackers and guerrillas, it was a risky undertaking for any man to make the trip. Joseph was entirely ignorant of the conditions and eagerly started out on horseback. He completed his task and returned safely with worthwhile knowledge, which no other man then possessed, of every county in the state. Real estate men found the information he could give them of great value.

Even during his hard experiences he had been a great reader, and he now began to study law, his late journeyings having naturally given him an insight into some of its phases. In 1868, four years after he had landed in this country, he was admitted to the bar. Ambitious and full of energy as he was, he soon found that life as a young lawyer was altogether too tame for him. Gladly, therefore, he accepted the post of reporter on the *Westliche Post*, a daily newspaper of which Carl Schurz was at that time the editor. So well did Mr. Pulitzer succeed in this new undertaking that before long he became managing editor and obtained a proprietary interest in the paper. He was never afraid of anyone's opinion and never hesitated to say what he believed as to the right or wrong of any public affair.

The tide of fortune had now definitely turned for Joseph Pulitzer. He had found what he could do successfully, the work which later brought him fame and riches.

In 1869 he was elected a member of the Missouri Legislature, and in 1874 to the State Constitutional Convention. In 1872 he was a delegate to the Cincinnati Convention which nominated Horace Greeley to the presidency, and in 1880 he was a member of the platform committee of the Democratic National Convention. He forged ahead so rapidly that honors came to the immigrant and destitute lad of so short a time ago.

In 1878 he founded the *Post-Dispatch* by buying the *Dispatch* and uniting it with the *Evening Post*. This brought him a yearly income of $150,000, and as he was now thirty-six years old he decided to go to Europe for study and rest. But just then he learned that the New York *World* was for sale and, despite the warnings of his physician that health and eyesight might be sacrificed if he did not rest, the temptation was too great to be resisted. In the twenty-three years of its existence the *World* had not been much of a success, but Mr. Pulitzer soon made a change. With all the energy at his command he worked until he made it one of the leading papers of the country.

He has been called "a great journalistic force whether for good or evil." Unquestionably he had high ideals. The following words expressed his conception of a great newspaper:

> An institution which should always fight for progress and reform; never tolerate injustice or corruption; always fight demagogues of all parties; never belong to any party; always oppose privileged and public plunder; never lack sympathy with the poor; always remain devoted to the public welfare; never be afraid to attack wrong.

Unfortunately he, like many another man, did not always live up to his ideals; he permitted a notable disregard for truth in the news columns of the *World*. He also at times failed to observe the rights of privacy in his eagerness to obtain information that would attract popular attention, so that this part of the paper was often by no means a creditable production. However, it was frequently public-spirited in its editorials. In relation to a proposed government bond issued in 1893 he demanded that it be thrown open to the people at large at its real value, instead of being handed to a group of financiers who could reap a large profit and thus rob the government. To prove his honesty of purpose he offered a million dollars in gold for the bonds. He succeeded in his aim, for the public were given fair opportunity to purchase the bonds. Mr. Pulitzer did loyally live up to his ideals in regard to fighting against special rights and special classes and as champion of the oppressed. He insisted always upon liberty being a reality and not merely a name. Even an advertiser who paid a big price for his pages was not allowed to influence the editorial policy in the slightest degree.

As he had long expected, he was finally stricken with blindness, but his activity and energy did not lessen. His health by this time was broken and he suffered so greatly that he was compelled to live away from his family and friends much of the time, mainly on his yacht, for there he could secure the quiet he needed. He had three secretaries, whose duty it was to keep him fully posted as to what was happening all over the world. At breakfast they had to furnish him with a review of new books, plays, music, and art. At lunch they were expected to supply descriptions of important persons and events. He was continually absorbing knowledge and then dictating material for his paper or sending cablegrams to the office. Thus for years did he wonderfully control and really edit the *World*, although he rarely entered its offices.

In his adopted country Mr. Pulitzer had made millions of dollars and, while he was generous with his family and those who had served him, he was anxious to benefit his fellow citizens. He gave Columbia University two million dollars to establish a school of journalism, so that men and women writers might have special training for their work. This school has attracted world-wide attention and approval. He also provided the Pulitzer Scholarship Fund of $250,000 and funds for the support of three graduates of the school who should pass examinations with the highest honors, to enable them to spend a year in Europe studying political, social, and moral conditions. In all his planning for the School of Journalism, he said, his chief end in view was the welfare of the Republic.

He left an annual prize of a gold medal to be given for the most disinterested and meritorious public service rendered by any American newspaper during the year, and an annual prize of one thousand dollars to be awarded for an American novel depicting the wholesome atmosphere of American life and the highest standard of American manhood and womanhood.

To his sons and sons-in-law he left his capital stock in the two papers he had founded, enjoining upon them the duty of perpetuating the New York *World* which he had striven to conduct as a public institution from motives higher than mere gain.

To the Metropolitan Museum of Art in New York City he bequeathed $500,000, and to the Philharmonic Society a like sum.

Joseph Pulitzer died in 1911.

Augustus St. Gaudens

"You can do anything you please; it's the way you do it that makes the difference." That significant saying of Augustus St. Gaudens was well proven in all his work, for he was never satisfied until he had made it as nearly perfect as possible. It was this thought that led him, from boyhood up, to be so intensely active that, while apprenticed to a cameo cutter and working very hard all day at a monotonous, wearisome task, he yet devoted his evenings to the study of drawing in the free classes at the Cooper Institute. Appreciating the opportunity, he took hold with such vigor that he himself said: "I became a terrific worker, toiling every night until eleven o'clock, after the classes were over. Indeed, I became so exhausted with the confining work of cameo cutting by day and drawing by night, that in the morning Mother literally dragged me out of bed, pushed me over to the washstand, where I gave myself a cat's lick somehow or other, drove me to the table, administering breakfast, and tumbled me downstairs out into the street, where I awoke."

Augustus St. Gaudens' father was French and his mother was Irish, and he inherited from them a love of the beautiful, yet he was essentially American both in his way of thinking and in his art. He was born in Dublin in 1848 and was brought to this country in the same year. In New York city his father, Bernard St. Gaudens, opened a shop where he continued his trade of making French boots and shoes. He had the wisdom to ask his son, Augustus, what kind of work he preferred to do when, at the age of thirteen, he had to quit school. The boy's reply that he would like to do something which would help him to be an artist, added to the advice of Dr. Rea Agnew, who had recognized the talent in the youth's rough sketches upon neighboring walls, led to his apprenticeship to a French cameo cutter named Avet. Under the control of this violent-tempered man Augustus had a hard time for a few years. Then in a fit of temper Avet discharged the boy, who at once went home and told his father what had occurred. When Avet came to the house a few minutes later to get Augustus to return, the boy refused to go with him. His father, who had not realized what sort of man his son had been working for, approved of the boy's decision. Later he helped his son find employment with another cameo cutter, Jules Brethon, a man of very different disposition. His evenings were now spent at the National Academy of Design instead of at the Cooper Institute.

The stirring days of the Civil War, with the recruiting of troops and the excitement attending the election of Abraham Lincoln, with a sight of that hero himself, made upon the lad indelible impressions of patriotism which later doubtless helped his work on the statues of our national heroes.

In 1867 his father offered Augustus a steerage passage to Europe, and the young man arrived in Paris with $100 saved from his wages. There, earning his living by cameo cutting in the afternoons, he devoted his mornings and evenings to study at the Petite Ecole and, later, under Jouffroy at the Ecole des Beaux Arts. He endured these long hours of work by frequent athletic exercises, swimming and walking excursions.

When in 1870 war was declared between France and Prussia the inclination of St. Gaudens to enlist on the side of France was very strong, but a pleading letter from his mother decided him to give up the idea, and he went to Rome, where for about four years he struggled with poverty while pushing his studies. He produced his first statue—that of Hiawatha "pondering, musing on the welfare of his people"—, but it was only through the orders given him by an American, Montgomery Gibbs, that he was able to secure enough money to have the figure cast. Back in New York for a brief period he did not at first find it easy to get worthwhile commissions, but an order for a bust of Senator Evarts encouraged him.

After another visit to Rome, he returned again to

the United States in 1875 and for a time had to take up teaching as a livelihood. A fortunate thing happened when he came in touch with the artist, John La Farge, for he said himself that the intimacy between them spurred him to higher endeavor. Good luck followed, for Governor Morgan secured for him the order for a statue of Admiral Farragut. It certainly was a triumph, for five of the committee voted to give the commission to a sculptor of high distinction, and he won by only one vote. Mr. La Farge also commissioned him to execute some bas-reliefs for St. Thomas Church, New York. In 1887 St. Gaudens helped to found the Society of American Artists. This Society was important, reflecting as it did a vital change in American sculpture and painting, which hitherto had been very conventional in style.

He married shortly thereafter, and he and his wife started again for Paris, where for three years he worked on the bas-reliefs, which when sent to Mr. La Farge were said by him to be "a living work of art." The Farragut statue was also completed, and then St. Gaudens returned to New York and took up his work definitely as an American sculptor. In his studio he gathered about him a circle of men who became admirers and life-long friends. Among the group were Stanford White, Charles F. McKim, H. H. Richardson, John La Farge, and others. While the result of his foreign studies was evident in his work, he used his training skillfully in establishing a distinctive American style and was the first artist to lead sculpture away from an imitation of the classic Greek forms. His Farragut statue is a "figure instinct at every point with the energy and strength of a man fronting perils in the open air amid great winds and under a vast sky."

His medallion work was most charming, very delicate and beautiful. The Robert Louis Stevenson medallion in St. Giles' Church, Edinburgh, is one of the finest examples. "He delighted in giving a clear, even forcible impression of the personality before him. It is portraiture for the sake of truth and beauty, not for the sake of technique."

Fourteen years of his life were given largely to the modeling of the monument to Robert Gould Shaw in Boston. There were times when he dropped work on it for the fulfillment of many other commissions; at other times he worked arduously upon a high scaffolding in the hot summers, seriously injuring his health. This monument is generally considered to be one of his greatest works in imaginative power, skill of composition, and perfection of technical detail. It was characteristic of St. Gaudens to spare himself no pains if thereby he might improve his work. Shaw had been a young Bostonian, "killed in action while leading his regiment—the 54th Massachusetts—of colored men led by white officers. Across the relief march the troops to the rhythm of the drum beat; there is a martial animation, but in the faces is the tense look of anticipation of the impending battle. Occupying the center of the panel, Shaw rides beside his men, an expression of sadness on his face. Above, floats a figure to which the artist gave no name, but which his interpreters have called Fame and Death."

St. Gauden's statue of Abraham Lincoln in Chicago is universally beloved, for it reveals the very soul of the great emancipator as he lives in the hearts of millions of people. "Simplicity is its predominating characteristic." "The tall, ungainly figure embodies in its attitude and in every hanging fold of the unfitted garments, the spirit of infinite tenderness, melancholy and strength."

The Logan and the Sherman monuments are both fine interpretations of the men they represent. General Logan rides with "the air of a conqueror. The body seems a living thing." The Sherman statue "is infused with the spirit of invincible determination."

Other notable works of this great sculptor are his "Puritan," which illustrates his aptitude in the presentation of a bygone personality, and his statue of Philips Brooks, which so well depicts the noble spirit of the man. But his chef d'oeuvre is the Adams memorial in the Rock Creek Cemetery near Washington, D.C. Commissioned by Henry Adams in memory of

his wife, the weary repose of the figure conveys a feeling of spiritual exhaustion and reveals "the sense of
doubt that is the tragedy of the modern mind." It has
been called "the finest thing of its kind ever produced
by an American sculptor, and an achievement which
modern Europe has not surpassed."

St. Gaudens was appointed one of the committee to
lay out the World's Fair grounds at Chicago, and he
personally designed the figure of Columbus in front
of the Administration Building. He was always interested in furthering the cause of American art. He
helped largely in founding the American Academy of
Fine Arts in Rome, and in developing the artistic
beauty of the National Capitol at Washington.

Honors began to press in upon him. Harvard, Yale
and Princeton gave him degrees. At Paris in 1900 he
was awarded the medal of honor, and at Buffalo a special medal was given him by his fellow artists who
"sought lovingly to exalt him as the master of them
all." In 1904 he was elected honorary foreign acade-
mician of the Royal Academy of London, and the
French government made him an officer of the Legion
of Honor and a corresponding member of the Society
of Fine Arts. But ever the United States grew more
dear to him. "No native-born sculptor was ever more
American than he, and none has ever succeeded in
bodying forth, in stone or bronze, such magnificent

visions, such sympathetic and powerful presentations of the nobility of American manhood." "Although of foreign birth and for many years resident abroad, he remained as distinctly American in his art as if he had come from a long line of native ancestors."

Jacob A. Riis

IN the quaint old town of Ribe, on the Danish sea-coast, a boy named Jacob A. Riis was born in 1849. When he was fifteen, to the great disappointment of his father, who was senior master in the Latin school at Ribe, he decided to become a carpenter. At the end of four years he received the certificate of the guild of his trade in Copenhagen. Shortly afterward he sailed for America, arriving in New York in 1870.

It was not easy for him to get work in New York, so he joined a gang of men going to Brady's Bend on the Allegheny River, where he started to build huts for the miners. That was followed by brickmaking and by work in a lumberyard. He had various unfortunate experiences in which he knew not how to earn enough for either food or lodging. Often he slept in doorways and suffered much because of insufficient clothing. He wandered from place to place, getting a job now and then, oftentimes hungry and often cheated out of his earnings.

After three years of this sort of thing he was fortu-nate in being offered employment as a reporter in New

York city. This was the beginning of his success. He spoke out of a hard experience when he said: "As to battling with the world, that is good for a young man, much better than to hang on to somebody for support. When you have fought your way through a tight place, you are the better for it. I am afraid that is not the case where you are shoved through."

Jacob Riis was a man of overflowing vitality and great energy, who, when he saw a wrong, was immediately seized with an intense desire to set it right. Sometimes this brought him trouble, but that in no way abated his ardor to make the world better.

An opportunity to become editor and then the owner of the South Brooklyn *News* naturally appealed to a man of his type. After becoming his own editor, reporter, publisher, and advertising agent, he exerted all his energy in making his paper "go."

Two things of great importance in his life occurred about this time. He was converted to Methodism at a revival meeting and decided to devote himself to a war against evil, villainy, and corruption of all sorts. And he received good news from Denmark. He had been sorely troubled by lack of letters from home, his anxiety being augmented by the fact that from boyhood he had set his heart upon winning the love of the daughter of a wealthy man in his native town. Since his absence from Ribe she had become engaged to another man. Shortly before Mr. Riis became an editor, however, he received word that her fiancé had died. Thereupon he sent a loving letter telling her of his unchanged love. The summer and fall had passed, but no word of any sort had reached him from his home town. At last, to his great joy, the message came for which he had been so ardently longing, the promise that made his stormy life full of happiness. Fortunately he had a chance soon after this to sell his paper for five times the amount he had paid for it and, after disposing of it, he took the first steamer for Denmark. Three months later he brought his bride to America.

For several months Mr. Riis earned their support by advertising merchandise by means of a stereopticon. But he was desirous of becoming a reporter on one of the metropolitan newspapers and finally succeeded in obtaining a position on the New York *Tribune*. It was hard work with little pay, not enough to live on. After some time he was assigned to police headquarters on Mulberry Street, where he found his lifework. It is interesting to note that Mr. Riis confessed to being almost afraid of the hard task before him, but in his characteristic way he said: "I commended my work and myself to the God of battles who gives victory, and I took hold. If I were to find that I could not put the case before Him who is the source of all right and justice, I should decline to go into the fight." The secret of Mr. Riis's success in his reform work is doubtless to be found in that decision. It was characteristic also that he did not wait until his return home to tell his wife, but before he began his new work he telegraphed her, "Got staff appointment. Police headquarters. Twenty-five dollars a week. Hurrah."

Out of the experiences he met in this new task he became familiar with the terrible conditions existing in the slums of New York city, and he did not rest until he had brought them to the attention of the public to have them remedied. He was a very thorough man in all his work. One summer there was fear of an epidemic of cholera. Picking up the weekly analysis of the water of the Croton River, the source of the city water supply, he noticed that for two weeks there had been "just a trace of nitrates" in it. His suspicions were aroused, and he at once questioned the health department chemist. He received only an evasive reply. Within an hour Mr. Riis had learned that nitrates were indications of sewage contamination, and he realized the peril. He spent a week following to its source every stream that discharged into the Croton River and photographing evidence of what he discovered. He told his story in the newspapers, illustrating it with his pictures. The city was startled, and the board of health sent inspectors to the watershed; their report was that things were much worse than Mr. Riis had claimed. The city took preventive action at once, at the cost of several million dollars.

Interesting as the story is, space permits only a brief

summary of the good things in the accomplishment
of which Mr. Riis was the moving spirit. He persisted
in showing the dreadful conditions in the police lodg-
inghouses, where dirty tramps and castaways, old and
young, lay at night on planks or on the stone floor and
then went out in the morning carrying the seeds of
disease to the homes where they begged for alms. Finally by a change in the laws the care of vagrants was
taken out of the hands of the police, and provision was
made for the care of the honest, homeless poor. Separate prisons for women, with police matrons in
charge, also resulted from the investigations he made.

With a camera Mr. Riis took evidence of the over-
crowding in the tenements in Mulberry Bend. To cite
but one instance, fifteen people were found living in a
room which should have held only four or five at the
most. There was no pretense at beds. The lodgers slept
there for "five cents a spot." In the twenty years that
Mr. Riis was a reporter in that neighborhood, not a
week passed without a crime or murder. At last, after
his long fight, the city bought the Bend, and the old
houses were torn down. A small park was placed there,
and the section that had been noted for its crime and
wickedness became the most orderly in the city.

Realizing the effectiveness of his newspaper and
magazine articles, publishers asked him to write in
book form. His first response was entitled, *How the
Other Half Lives*. This was followed by *The Children*

of the Poor, The Battle with the Slums, Children of the Tenements, his autobiography, *The Making of an American,* and *Theodore Roosevelt, Citizen.*

He was very much stirred by the sight of the little children in the East Side factories. False certificates asserting they had reached the age of fourteen were permitted because of lack of birth registration. With characteristic thoroughness Mr. Riis learned from a doctor that the latest age at which a child cuts his "dog teeth" is twelve years. Then he visited the factories and obliged the children to let him see their teeth; if they had not their "dog teeth," that was conclusive evidence that they were not yet fourteen. The investigation resulted in a change in the law that freed the children from factory work.

Good teaching and decent schools were other demands made by Mr. Riis. He was constantly working for the good of the boys and girls. Too many schools were overcrowded, and there was insufficient light for the children to see slates and blackboards. Dark basement rooms, thirty by fifty-two feet, full of rats, were the only playgrounds for a thousand children. In the whole of Manhattan there was but one outdoor playground attached to a public school, and that was an old burial ground. Mr. Riis's showing of the facts aroused the city. The whole school system was remodeled, and sixty new schoolhouses were built. The Playground Association was formed, and small parks were created to let daylight into the slums. This resulted in the reduction of the death rate from 26.32 per thousand in 1887 to 19.53 in 1897.

If you wish to learn more of it, read Mr. Riis's book, *The Making of an American*. All this and much else were the outcome of the patient efforts of a poor immigrant, who came to America from Denmark at the age of twenty-one, with all the odds against him at the start, but of whom ex-President Theodore Roosevelt has said "he was the most useful American of his day. He came the nearest to the ideal of an American citizen." It has also been said of him that "no man has ever more vitally and faithfully expressed and interpreted the American spirit. He was a brother to all men and especially to the unfortunate."

His love for his native land was deep and loyal. His enthusiasm for all that was connected with it was strong, and he never permitted any slight put upon its national flag to go unrebuked. But when he lay ill at the home of a friend in Denmark, after he had gone home to visit his mother once more, he suddenly saw from the window a ship flying the United States flag. "Gone," he said, "were illness, discouragement, and gloom. Forgotten weakness and suffering. I shouted, laughed, and cried by turns. I knew then that it was my flag; that I had become an American in truth. And I thanked God, and, like the man sick with the palsy, arose from my bed and went home healed."

Jacob A. Riis died in 1914, but his memory is kept alive through the many public projects which have been named for him, including, among others, a popular bathing beach, several housing developments, and the Henry Street Settlement House and Nursery School which he was instrumental in organizing.

Samuel Gompers

IN 1863, a boy aged thirteen entered the United States as an immigrant from London. His only schooling was obtained in a day school from his sixth to his tenth year, with four years of evening school later. But he was eager to learn, often forgetting to eat in his absorption in his books. This boy grew to be one of the most influential men in the Labor movement of his day and was given the title of "Labor Statesman of the World."

Once an object of supercilious contempt, laughed at by capitalists and government officials for his visions of the future status of the working man and for his untiring efforts to secure fair treatment for him, Samuel Gompers, as president of the American Federation of Labor, was the acknowledged leader of nearly three million men organized in labor unions. A few months before his death, the London *Times* devoted an editorial to a eulogy of him, and another influential journal said that "no man in the United States except President Wilson wielded such power as did Mr. Gompers." Here is an illustration of his influence: A former Commissioner of Indian Affairs prepared plans for a series of public improvements on a certain reservation, proposing to use Indian labor at the current hourly wage. As most of the Indians had to come a long distance from home, it was found necessary to substitute a ten-hour day for the legal eight, with only five working days in the week. Someone called attention to this plan as a violation of the statute limiting hours of work done by government employees. The Commissioner therefore endeavored to procure an amendment making the statute nonapplicable to work done by Indians on their own reservations. When he brought his measure before the appropriate Congressional Committee he was asked, "Have you seen Gompers?" There appeared to be no alternative, so Gompers was consulted, and he promptly vetoed the project which, therefore, had to be abandoned.

After World War I, at a great gathering in Chicago attended by governors of a dozen states, Samuel Gompers received a hearty endorsement in appreciation of the work he had done to unite the labor leaders of Europe in wholehearted support of the Allied war efforts.

It was his quiet determination, his tenacity of purpose, that brought him to the place of honor and influence which he attained. Although born in London in 1850 he was a Hollander by descent. He attributed to his mother, whose parents, he said, were highly educated, his own love of study and his desire to benefit his fellow men.

His first impulse in the direction of the cause to which he devoted his life was received when, as a boy, he saw thousands of silk weavers in Spitalfields deprived, by the introduction of machinery, of work in the trade to which their fathers and grandfathers had belonged. They were marching under banners that declared, "We are starving."

"Labor organization is the bulwark of democracy" was his theory and practical faith. He began early to work toward its realization. A cigar-maker at fifteen, he helped to organize the first cigar-maker's union of New York. Ten years later he was elected its secretary. He also served as its president for six successive terms. For thirty-six years he worked at his trade, afterwards devoting his time and strength to the betterment of the condition of the working classes.

In 1881 his local union took part in the formation of a national organization. It was a day of small beginnings, for there were but seven delegates, of whom Mr. Gompers was one. He was its president continuously, with the exception of one term. Under his efficiency and personal power its membership rose to nearly three million. At an annual meeting of the American Federation of Labor in 1908 his rule of action, "Partisan to no political party but partisan to a principle," was approved by the organization. He urged upon working people "the imperative necessity and solemn duty of resisting by all means at their command the tendency on the part of the employers and princes of finance to establish in some form or other in this country political and judicial despotism."

When World War I began, his devotion to democracy inspired him with enthusiasm for the cause of the Allies. He was eager to have Labor help America show herself to be efficient in war as in peace. It was an indication of the force of his personality that he secured from the Federation a pledge of undivided support in carrying forward the war to a successful conclusion, but he demonstrated also his skill as a strategist in demanding, as a fundamental prerequisite to co-operation, recognition by the government of employees as a group having common interests; thus maintaining the union principle. The result was a closer relation between Labor and the Federal Administration than had ever existed previously. It has been said that Mr. Gompers was a member of the President's Cabinet in all but the name. He furthered the creation of a Federal Department of Labor, and it became the chief agency of the government for dealing with labor disputes relating to wartime production. Mr. Gompers' office was of great influence in supplying initiative for important decisions. In a speech at Buffalo, New York, President Wilson took occasion to speak of Gompers' "patriotic courage, his large vision, his statesmanlike sense and mind that knew how to pull in harness."

For many years Mr. Gompers endeavored to secure for labor unions exemption from the operation of the Sherman Antitrust Act, and also from injunction by the courts of law, and he was finally successful. He argued that

> business cannot be property and therefore whenever the courts issue injunctions which undertake to regulate our relations with our employers or those from whom we may or may not purchase commodities, such courts are trespassing upon relations which are personal relations and with which equity power has no concern.

Gompers was not a Socialist and it was his constant endeavor to prevent the Federation of Labor from endorsing Socialistic policies. He frankly said that he was at variance with the philosophy of Socialism and its doctrines. "Economically they are unsound; socially they are wrong; industrially they are an impossibility." He did not approve of force or violence; despite his ardor for the success of the war for democracy, he was a pacifist, a peacemaker. His declaration to the Chicago Federation on strikes was:

> We cannot win by thuggery or violence. Brutality only grows. If we had to win by that method, it would be better to lose. Violence and thuggery only hurt our movement. . . . When compulsion is used, only re-

sentment is aroused and the end is not gained. Only through moral suasion and appeal to men's reason can a movement succeed.

The I.W.W. received no support from him, for he did not agree with their theory that one class must be uprooted to give place to another. Give the working men good wages, homes and living conditions, he said, and there would be no occasion to disturb anyone. "There would not have to be any labor unions if every employer were like Henry Ford," was his declaration.

The personality of Mr. Gompers is, of course, largely revealed in what has already been said of him, but it is interesting to have a pen picture of him. He was short and heavily built, with massive head and broad shoulders; his hair was long and gray, brushed back severely from his forehead. He wore spectacles over eyes that were keen but kindly. Determination and benignancy were both evident in his features. Englishmen were surprised that he did not match up to the press portraits of the labor boss; they noted that he did not wear any heavy gold chain or gaudy vest, or carry a half-chewed cigar stub tilting upward from his lips. He was quiet in manner and unobtrusive in appearance.

Deliberation was a prominent characteristic and he was cautious in the extreme. William Hard described him as going out on a new idea as cautiously as an elephant going over a new bridge. He proved himself to be an incorruptible leader and a master strategist. His methods of accomplishing his aims were by preparation, patience, conciliation, and delay. In debate he waited until his opponent had exhausted all his arguments and then adroitly turned back the same arguments. He knew well how to concentrate all his efforts upon a single purpose; it was the secret of his brilliant career. He allowed nothing to divert his mind from his one aim of helping the working man to better his condition. "Gompersian forcefulness" is the name given by one writer to his way of steadily pushing forward to his goal. An Englishman says: "The most persistent journalist could not sidetrack him where he did not want to go. He quietly, so to speak, shunted himself back onto the main line, pushing the journalist before him."

For a man who had little schooling, it is remarkable that he acquired such correct use of the English language. He was thoroughly familiar with the best literature in three languages besides English, and he had unusual ability in writing pamphlets. He lectured at Harvard, Cornell, Michigan, and Wisconsin universities.

Although finally receiving a yearly salary of $7,000, as president of the Federation of Labor, Mr. Gompers was by no means even a well-to-do man, for he gave so largely to union men who were in need that his own family were sometimes decidedly limited in their expenditures. For the first four years of his presidency he received nothing; for the next five, he had $1,200 a year. Knowing his poverty previous to his taking office with the Federation, Governor Hill of New York offered him the post of Commissioner of Arbitration at a salary of $3,000 a year; yet, though he was earning scarcely twenty dollars a week, he refused the offer. Other advantageous positions were suggested to him, among them a nomination to Congress and a place on the Industrial Commission, but one and all were declined, a striking evidence of his steadfast adherence to his life purpose. The records of a manufacturing association gave proof that he was also offered $4,500 in cash and a sinecure for life, which was likewise refused. Is it any wonder that he was devotedly loved by thousands of American working men?

Mr. Gompers was active to the last. While on a visit to Mexico City, in the cause of labor, he was suddenly stricken. A special train rushed him to the border, but he grew worse and died in San Antonio, Texas, on December 13, 1924. He was seventy-four years old. Tributes from all political parties and from all over the world testified to the high esteem in which he was held.

Felix Adler

"A PERSONALITY of spiritual majesty and light; one does him unconscious reverence." This is a tribute that not one person only, but many would give to Dr. Adler after his fifty years of devotion to a great cause—the cause of moral righteousness.

When as a young man Felix Adler broke away from the Jewish church to begin a noble lifework in accordance with his intellectual belief and moral insight, there must have been a strange wrench to himself, to his family, and to the large body of synagogue members who knew him as the able son of his revered father. Brought up in the traditions and faith of an orthodox Jewish home, with his father a devout and scholarly German Rabbi, who had become leader of the great Temple Emanu El of New York city, Felix had been destined for the Jewish ministry.

He was born in Alzey, Germany, in 1851, and for twenty years of his life German as well as Jewish influences were around him. Because of recognition of his exceptional ability and the belief that he was gifted to become a leader and teacher of men, Felix

Adler was sent to Columbia University and then to study at Berlin and Heidelberg, where he obtained his Ph.D. in 1873. He returned to America but not to follow in his father's footsteps. Many influences affected his clear thinking and earnest spirit. He had known Emerson at home and studied Kant abroad. It was the time when higher Biblical criticism and the principle of evolution were bringing light to many minds. Adler's conception of life and truth and his passion for sincerity could not allow him to hold to rituals, ceremonies, and many Mosaic Laws, or to a God of a chosen and superior people. He believed all races were equal and interdependent; he had faith in the high worth of every human being. He would have a social and spiritual service on a purely ethical basis.

For two years he served as Professor of Hebrew and Oriental Literature at Cornell University. In 1876 Dr. Adler returned to New York city and established the Society for Ethical Culture amid considerable controversy. It was first organized under the name of "Union for the Higher Life," among a group of young men friends, and was based on three tacit assumptions: sex-purity; the principle of devoting the surplus of one's income beyond that required for one's own genuine needs to the elevation of the working class; and, thirdly, continued intellectual development.

The society grew in numbers and power with many

prominent Jews becoming members. However, Dr. Adler's ideal has been nonsectarian, interracial, and interreligious, positing ethics as the basis of all religions, and many of the members of the society have been non-Jewish. In it theology has no place, and the differences of Judaism and Christianity are set aside. There is no formal creed. It dedicates itself simply to "promoting the knowledge, the love, and the practice of the right." The words over the New York Meeting House are these: "The place where men seek the Highest is holy ground."

No man could be more reverent or less partisan in spirit than was Felix Adler. A story is told of his being in a group of ministers one day, and a conversation was started on what question each would ask if Jesus came into the room. After several questions had been suggested, Dr. Adler was asked what he would say. His reply was, "I should be silent, lost in wonder and awe." (In his writings he refers to Jesus as the highest of the Hebrew prophets.)

Through many years he gave discourses on Sunday morning to the Society of Ethical Culture. Dr. Henry Neumann, in speaking of the Ethical Movement, says it has been religious from the beginning. He quotes from Emerson, "The progress of religion is steadily to its identity with morals," and adds, "Rationalistic objections to dogmas were not the chief occasion why Felix Adler went out from the faith of his fathers.

The leading impulse was the need of a new consecrating influence."

This "consecrating influence" developed into a moral enthusiasm. The right for the right's sake was its basis. It would be an injustice to attempt to outline Dr. Adler's *Ethical Philosophy of Life* in this brief sketch—his various writings and especially his book under this title must give that insight. An extract or two may reveal something of his character and thought; he insisted that life must be one of constant advance.

> The supremacy of the moral end of life above all other ends, the sufficiency of man for the pursuit of that end, the increase of moral truth to be expected from loyalty in this pursuit—these are the three tenets, if we may call them so, of an ethical creed. . . . By ceaseless efforts to live the good life we maintain our moral sanity. Not from without, but from within, flow the divine waters that renew the soul. The ethical element of religion has ever been its truly vital and quickening force. It is this which lends such majesty to the speeches of the Prophets, which gives such ineffable power and sweetness to the words of Jesus. Has this ethical element become less important in our age? Has the need of accentuating it become less imperative? Today, in the estimation of many, science and art are taking the place of religion. But science and art alike are inadequate to build up character and to furnish binding rules of conduct. . . .

Let us produce, through the efficacy of a better moral life and of a deeper moral experience, a surer faith in the ultimate victory of the good.

In discussing "The Moral Ideal," Dr. Adler said:

The moral ideal should be conceived as a supreme society rather than as a supreme individual. . . . The creative endeavor to realize, or approximate to the realization of the infinite organic scheme, in terms of actual social progress replaces worship in the older sense as homage toward a single being regarded as embodying in himself the totality of moral excellence. Union with the infinite is the experience within oneself of the compelling impulse that issues from the idea of infinite organism, and the sense that the worth of life consists, despite the tragic shortcomings, in unremitting effort to yield obedience to the impulse.

Societies for Ethical Culture have spread to a few other cities, but in half a century their membership has not grown to large numbers. This is probably due to the fact that there is a cold intellectual quality, one might almost say a hardness, about their belief and their services. While their author had a passion for righteousness, it was so restrained by a calm philosophy that there is little emotional contagion.

The Ethical Culture School established by the New York Society for Ethical Culture began as a kindergarten in 1878—the first free kindergarten to be opened in New York city. The school soon grew to over nine hundred pupils and later expanded even further. Eventually it included a normal school and a pre-vocational Art High School besides other high schools.

A number of pioneer social enterprises must be credited to the New York Society for Ethical Culture: the free kindergarten, when this means of education was little appreciated or even known by many persons; manual training for the elementary school grades; district nursing when it was introduced into this country; festivals and dramatic presentations which later led to civic festivals; organization of classes for adult education.

Felix Adler said:

> If education is to improve mankind, the first imperative necessity is that education itself be improved. . . . To improve human conditions it is necessary to improve human beings. The converse also is true: better people to achieve better conditions, better conditions to have better people—the effort of change must be undertaken from both ends.

In the announcement of the Ethical Culture Pre-professional School, he emphasized:

> Any plan for the creation of a better world to live in, as peace instead of war, the spirit of coöperation between employers and workers, and more of beauty and enduring felicity in sex relations, is not feasible

unless individual men and women are educated to meet the requirements of the plan.

Felix Adler labored with Theodore Roosevelt, Jacob Riis, and others for tenement reform and municipal welfare in New York city. He gave himself to the cause of rescuing children from child labor. For seventeen years and up to 1921, he was chairman of the National Child Labor Committee, which, as he said, "seeks to put an end to the national disgrace of child mistreatment and at the same time to promote every enterprise that looks toward a wiser and more efficient education of our youth." This organization has taken thousands of children out of the mills and in later years has turned its special attention to securing freedom and better conditions for children who labor on farms. Dr. Adler said:

[In considering] what it is at bottom that accounts for so monstrous a thing as the use of child labor, especially among a people like ours,—so quick to resent oppression, so readily sympathetic with suffering, I have come to the conclusion that here we come upon the seamy side of our evaluation of efficiency. We are keen to bring things to pass, we put our very selves into work and so we come to estimate the human factor, not in terms of what a man is, but of what he produces, and we come to think of a little child, not as it is, a germ of spiritual life as yet not unfolded, a precious asset for the future of the world, but we are prone to think of the child in terms of what even these little hands, this weary little body can be coerced to produce. The movement against Child Labor, therefore, has had for me a great significance of making an inroad in this country on the habit of sacrificing personality to the work; if we can make people respect the really human factor in the child, they will be more prepared to respect the same in the adult.

Dr. Adler's interpretation of a citizen is "one who helps to realize the purpose for which this nation exists." For many years he was professor of Political and Social Ethics at Columbia University. He was exchange professor at the University of Berlin in 1908–09, and Hibbert lecturer at Oxford in May, 1923. He was president of the Eastern Division of the American Philosophical Association in 1928.

In his many writings he set forth with great clarity his ethical and philosophical conceptions at the time they were written: *Creed and Deed* in 1877, *Ethics of the Political Situation* in 1884. Helpful counsel is given in Dr. Adler's *Moral Instruction of Children* (1902), and his high conception of marriage is shown in *Marriage and Divorce* (1905). His *Religion of Duty,* and *Essentials of Spirituality* were written about this time; *The World Crisis and Its Meaning* in 1915; and *An Ethical Philosophy of Life* a few years later. *Life and Destiny* is a collection of extracts from Dr. Adler's lectures and is full of helpful suggestions;

The Reconstruction of the Spiritual Ideal (1923) is the crown of his ideas.

He was the chief editor of *The Standard*, the organ of the American Ethical Union, "To promote ethical thinking and to encourage better ways of living."

Dr. Adler's contribution to the world was one of high spiritual appeal. His moral ideal was so exalted that he was, inevitably, discouraged by the disparity between that ideal and the real world in which he worked. At the end of his career he said:

> I look back on my life and its net results. I have seen spiritual ideals and the more clearly I see them, the wider appears the distance between them and the empirical conditions, the changes I could effect in those conditions. I have worked in social reform, and the impression I have been able to make now seems to me so utterly insignificant as to make my early sanguine aspirations appear pathetic. . . . I look lastly into my heart, my own character, and the effort I have made to fuse the discordant elements to achieve a genuine integrity there, and I find the disappointment there the deepest of all.

Yet, it has been said that Dr. Adler's real greatness did not lie in any of the things that he did, but in the man himself, in his *being*. Though he died on April 24, 1933, the influence of his powerful personality remains, like that of the great prophets, as a symbol of man's aspiration for moral righteousness.

Ottmar Mergenthaler

I N these days of the multiplicity of the printed page
we may well remember the man who invented the
linotype, which enables an operator to print four or
five times faster than it can be done by hand. The inventor of this machine came to the United States from
Germany in 1872. He was born in May, 1854, at
Bietigheim, located some twenty miles from Stutt-
gart. His father was a teacher, his mother also belonged to a family which for long years had practiced
that profession. The boy was educated at his father's
school. At home he was not allowed much time for
play, for he had to help cook the meals, wash dishes,
build fires during the winter and take care of the garden in the summer. The year round he was expected
to feed the pigs and cattle.

At the age of fourteen Ottmar was supposed to
begin his training as a teacher, but that occupation
did not offer any attractions for him. He had a special
liking for mechanics, having kept clocks in repair and
made models of animals out of wood. He chose to become an apprentice to a Mr. Hahl, a brother of his

stepmother and a maker of watches and clocks. The terms were four years' service without wages. He was also to pay a small premium and provide his own tools. Board and lodging were to be furnished by his employer. Ottmar had a pleasant home with Mr. Hahl, and he enjoyed his work as well as the company of the other young men workers. He developed unusual skill and mechanical talent and succeeded so well that wages were paid him a year before the expiration of his apprenticeship. The rarity of the young man's ability is evident from the fact that this was the first time in a business life of over thirty years that Mr. Hahl had found occasion so to recognize talent in any youth.

Ottmar sought to improve all opportunities open to him in the night school, getting in this way his first lessons in mechanical drawing, which later proved to be of much advantage to him in the drafting of his inventions. In 1872, at the close of his four years' apprenticeship, he had to decide where to locate for starting a business on his own account. The close of the Franco-Prussian War had left conditions in Germany very unsatisfactory. There was a large amount of unemployment, and increased military duties were causing many young men to leave the country. Ottmar therefore decided to do likewise, and applied to August Hahl, son of his late employer and a maker of electrical instruments in Washington, D.C., for a loan of passage money to be repaid by working in his factory. The money was promptly sent, and Mergenthaler landed in Baltimore in October, 1872, going at once to Washington.

Electrical instruments were unfamiliar to him, but he soon mastered their workings, and within two years he was made foreman of the shop, even acting as business manager when Mr. Hahl was absent. The United States Signal Service had been established only a short time earlier, and Mergenthaler's work was largely the making of standard instruments for it. For this he appeared to have special fitness. Washington was a place where inventor's models, which were required whenever anyone filed an application for a patent, were particularly built, and this brought Mergenthaler into contact with many inventors and stimulated his own talent in that direction. In August, 1876, his attention was attracted to the model of a writing machine. He examined it and saw how to remedy its defects. He was commissioned to build a machine of full size, and he did so in 1877. But though much improved, it never could be a real success. Then an attempt was made to have stereotypy take the place of lithography in the making of an impression machine, but after several efforts Mergenthaler told his employers that it could never be brought to perfection.

In January, 1883, J. O. Clephane and others who were interested in backing these various attempts, asked Mergenthaler to try to devise a machine to take the place of typesetting done by hand, which was a slow and laborious process. On New Year's Day he dissolved the partnership with Mr. Hahl, which had existed for two years, and started in business for himself. Settling in Baltimore he proceeded to work out the desires of his Washington friends. His own plan was to imprint a matrix—a slight bar of metal in which is sunk a character to serve as a mold—line by line, each line being justified, or spaced, as a unit. Experiments were tried, but without success, until one day the thought came into his mind: why not stamp the matrices or molds into type bars and pour fluid metal into them, as is done by typefounders? In this case he desired to do the whole process in one machine.

His backers needed persuasion before they were willing to endorse the new idea, but finally they gave the order to Mergenthaler to build two machines according to his plan. In 1884, when the first of these machines was ready to be tested, a dozen spectators came to see the operation. Everything went off well. The line of type was composed by touching a keyboard. Then the fluid metal was poured over it and a finished linotype, shining like silver, dropped from the machine, while each matrix was sent back to its own receptacle. All was done within fifty seconds. It was a notable event in the history of printing.

During the next two years the inventor improved

and simplified his linotype. In February, 1885, he exhibited a much improved machine at the Chamberlain Hotel in Washington, printers from all over the world being interested. A banquet followed in honor of the inventor's great achievement. But still later Mergenthaler saw that to make it more perfect he must give visibility to its motions so that the operator could see what he was doing. He also aimed to produce a single-matrix machine. Other inventors were at work on similar ideas, but the invention of Mergenthaler had points of excellence which gave it first place, chief of all being that the three processes of typesetting, typefounding, and stereotyping are combined in one machine. Whitelaw Reid, editor of the New York *Tribune,* gave the linotype its name. He was the first to use the new invention in printing his newspaper. At the close of 1886 a dozen of the machines were at work in the *Tribune* offices. The Chicago *Inter-Ocean* and the Louisville *Courier-Journal* also adopted it. In 1880 big profits were gained from the linotype. The New York *Tribune* saved within twelve months $80,000. And yet the inventor's royalty was only fifty dollars per machine.

Still Mergenthaler continued to make improvements until he had at last a wonderfully perfect machine. As it now stands, its method of working, briefly told, is as follows: The operator has before him the control of about 1500 matrices. Each matrix, or mold, is a small flat plate of brass which has on its outer edge an incised letter, and its upper end a series of teeth for distributing purposes. As the operator touches a key the letter desired is set free and glides in full view to its assembling place, which supplants the old-fashioned stick. In like manner each letter reaches its destination until the word is completed. Then the operator touches a key that inserts a space shaped like a double wedge. When the line of type is full, it is justified by moving a lever, and it is carried automatically to a mold where liquid metal is forced against the matrices and spaces. Then the line of type is ready to be printed. This slug, as it is called, in a moment is hard and cool enough to pass to a tray where other slugs are swiftly added to form a page or column ready for the printing press. A set of matrices often replaces a font of type weighing two hundred times as much. A section of the machine returns the matrices to their boxes as quickly as 270 a minute and unerringly, unless a matrix is bent by accident or otherwise injured. In a linotype three distinct operations go on together: composing one line, casting a second and distributing a third, so that the machine has a pace exceeding that at which an expert operator can finger his keys.

Since Mergenthaler's work was finished, his linotype has been adapted to composing books of the most exacting kind, mathematical treatises, and the like. It has also been arranged for printing in many languages, and for casting letters twice the ordinary length for use in newspaper headings.

Mergenthaler was beloved by all the men who worked for him. He was good to all of them and, no matter how humble their station, he always had a kind word for them and a friendly word to say of them.

Worn out from hard work, he contracted tuberculosis in 1894, and five years later he died, but not before he had been gladdened by recognition of his great ability by the award of a medal from the Cooper Institute of New York; the John Scott medal by the City of Philadelphia; and the Elliott Cresson gold medal by the Franklin Institute of Philadelphia.

Michael Pupin

AMERICA worked considerable transformation in a Serbian lad who ran away from his native land in 1874, and nine years later graduated from Columbia College, won a Ph.D. from Berlin in 1889, and within fifteen years from the time he landed became a member of the faculty of Columbia.

This lad, Michael Pupin by name, was born in Idvor, Hungary. He was descended from Serbian ancestors who had settled in the Province of Banat, north of the Danube. Complete political and spiritual freedom from the dominant Magyars had been promised them by the Austro-Hungarian Emperor, on the condition that they defend Austria against the Turks. And though they kept their word, the Emperor broke his by turning them over to Hungary and making them vassals of the Magyars. Michael Pupin long remembered the bitterness with which his father would say, "The Emperor has betrayed us. I will see that you never serve in his army."

As it happened, Michael did not serve in the Emperor's army. Before he had finished school at Prague, he ran away to America to avoid being conscripted and to see the country of "the greatest man who ever lived, Abraham Lincoln." To get to America young Michael sold his watch, his books and all of his clothes except those that he wore on the voyage. The proceeds from this sale, together with the money he had saved from his small allowance, brought him to the United States. When he arrived he had just five cents in his pocket.

Before admitting him to the United States, immigration officials asked if he had any friends in this country, and he replied, "Yes—Abraham Lincoln and Benjamin Franklin." The officials said, "You have chosen your friends wisely," and they allowed him to pass. He was hired by a Delaware farmer who treated him well. The daughter of the house taught him English in the evenings. But he came to the conclusion after a while that farming did not appeal to him, so he went to Philadelphia where his talents for drawing secured him a place with a photographer, retouching negatives. Later, he went to New York and took work in a cracker factory.

He had made good use of the short time he had been in this country for he was now able to read English with ease. He became interested in the scientific articles published in the *Sun*, a daily paper of New York, and he decided to get an education and become a scientist. It was a considerable undertaking but he was not afraid of the hard work involved. He had already been improving his opportunities and had read the speeches of Webster, Clay, Calhoun and Lincoln. The Gettysburg speech of President Lincoln he had committed to memory, as well as Bryant's "Thanatopsis." This was good training for his English, but he felt that his pronunciation was faulty, so he often went to the top gallery of the theater where he could hear Edwin Booth, Lawrence Barrett, and John McCullough. In the same year he began attending night school, taking lessons in drawing, physics, and chemistry.

When he was twenty he had saved $311 and he applied for a scholarship at Columbia College. When he was interviewed by the committee in charge, he recited whole pages of ancient Greek which he had laboriously memorized. One of the professors asked him why he had gone to so much trouble, and he replied, "Because I cannot afford not to get the scholarship." He got it, but of course he still had to earn money for his living expenses, so he worked at various jobs. During the first summer vacation he earned $75 besides his board, by haymaking in New Jersey. For the remainder of his college course he undertook coaching of fellow students. The indomitable perseverance of the young man is evident in the steadiness with which he pursued his aim of getting an education, for he triumphed over all difficulties and graduated from college in 1883. Then he went abroad on a fellowship that enabled him to study mathematics and physics at both Cambridge University and the University of Berlin.

Returning to America, this foreign-born young man who had so signally made good was appointed instructor in mathematical physics at Columbia. In 1892 he was made adjunct professor of mechanics, and in 1901 professor of electronics. Elected a member of the National Academy of Sciences in 1906, he was made director of the Phoenix Research Laboratories in 1911.

Today Professor Pupin is known the world over wherever electrical problems are being solved. He was a scientist who delighted to unravel complex problems. He made investigation simply because he desired to know things, not because with the knowledge gained he would have a commercial advantage, although he claimed "there is no worth-while purely scientific problem, the correct solution of which will not some day have a practical value." His discoveries in pure physics have frequently been the foundation on which others have built. His theory of selective tuning to separate mixed electrical operations, for instance, was completed two years before Marconi announced his wireless. As applied by Marconi, selective tuning made the reception of messages of different wave lengths possible. Professor Pupin also developed the principle and the apparatus for rectifying alternating electrical forces, thus laying the groundwork for the marvelous vacuum tube rectifier.

His most important practical contributions to the world of science were his researches in electrical resonance and the magnification of iron. In the early days of the telephone there was great trouble with interference by unaccountable buzzing, clicking, and humming noises on long distance wires. The difficulty was solved through the use of "Pupin's coil," a device consisting of insulated wire wound on very finely laminated iron cores encased in watertight boxes. He also invented a device for eliminating static interference in wireless transmission. And after Roentgen's famous discovery, Pupin developed the first X-ray for surgical work.

Pupin's work with his students was another source of value to the world, for he inspired them to do good and valuable work. He was a strong teacher, having not only intellectual power of unusually high degree but a personality that attracted. He had also a fine sense of humor and was a great athlete as well as a great scientist. He felt honored in being an American citizen, but he by no means forgot his native land and was always active in the interests of Serbia. At the outbreak of the Balkan war in 1912 he was appointed by the Serbian government honorary consul general at New York. In 1915 he organized among Columbia students relief workers for Serbia.

Not a few honors came to him: he was given the degree of Ph.D. by the University of Berlin; an honorary degree from Johns Hopkins; the Elliot Cresson medal for distinction in physics; the Hebert prize of the French Academy in physics, and the gold medal of the National Institute of Science. Thus the Serbian boy had made good in his adopted country.

In later years Professor Pupin wrote considerably on scientific subjects in the magazines, and in 1922 he published his autobiography, *From Immigrant to Inventor*. Of this book he says:

> The main object of my narrative was, and still is, to describe the rise of idealism in American science, and particularly in physical sciences and the related industries. . . . Why should a scientist who started his career as a Serbian immigrant speak of the idealism in American science when there are so many native-born American scientists who know more about this subject than I do? . . . I shall only point out now that there are certain psychological elements in the question which justify me in the belief that occasionally an immigrant can see things which escape the attention of the native. Seeing is believing; let him speak who has the faith, provided that he has a message to deliver.

The account of Michael Pupin's life and work is very simply written and is full of interest. In speaking of "scientific idealism," he says it is a "simple philosophy which cultivates a definite motive, a definite mental attitude, and a definite method of inquiry. The motive is the unselfish search of the eternal truth; the mental attitude is open-minded and unprejudiced interpretation of the language of nature; the method, one of inquiry, observation, experiment, and calculation."

This scientist was one of a group who believe that back of everything is a definite guiding principle which leads from chaos to cosmos. He says, "Science reveals Man as a being with a soul which is progressing more and more by degrees toward divinity in a universe of unbroken continuity. Science is leading us closer and closer to God. Science will strengthen religion. It has strengthened mine. I believe it will make better Christians of all men and women who try to understand its simple and beautiful laws because they are the laws of God."

Dr. Pupin died in New York city, March 12, 1935, in his seventy-seventh year.

Charles Proteus Steinmetz

A GREAT mind in a small body—he stood only four feet high and carried an enormous head between high shoulders—one of the world's greatest mathematicians, a mental dynamo. So was Charles Proteus Steinmetz described when he was professor of electrical engineering in Union College, Schenectady, N.Y., and the highly valued consulting engineer of the General Electric Company of the same city. Distinguished as he became, he belonged to a poor family in Breslau, Germany, where he was born on April 9, 1865. His father, a lithographer by trade but later a railroad employee, was determined that his son should be well educated and did everything in his power toward that end. In order to test fully his tastes and capabilities Charles took preparatory courses in medicine, political economy, mechanical engineering, and other studies in the University of Breslau. Finally he gave himself to full and comprehensive work in mathematics, higher chemistry, and electricity.

During his student days Steinmetz was arrested by the repressive German government for membership in a socialist club. Later he was released, but a fellow student was remanded for trial. Steinmetz obtained permission to bring his friend writing materials so that he might finish his doctor's thesis while in jail. He was also allowed to bring toilet articles, such as toothpaste. And his friend was permitted to have books, though each book that Steinmetz brought to the jail was rigorously inspected by a government agent before it was allowed in the prisoner's cell. After the trial at which this medical student was acquitted, the prosecuting agent was dismayed to discover that he had passed upon books whose blank pages were covered with invisible writing that the prisoner had been able to develop with a solution made from toothpaste and blotting paper. From suggestions thus made to him, he had been able to work out his defense. Steinmetz who had made the invisible ink and had planned the whole affair, found the country an unsafe place to stay in and escaped to Switzerland in 1888. A year later he emigrated to the United States.

Here he worked for a time at twelve dollars a week with Eickemeyer and Company at Yonkers, New York. While there his loneliness as a stranger in a strange land was relieved one evening by an acquaintance who invited him to his home for supper. In grateful recognition of this act of friendliness he later adopted a son of the poor family, and it is believed that he assisted in the education of others.

In 1894 after the General Electric Company had consolidated the Eickemeyer business with its own, the headquarters were transferred to Schenectady. Soon afterward Steinmetz became its Consulting Engineer at a salary which stood for some time at $100,-000 a year. In 1902 he also accepted the professorship of electrical engineering at Union College. The clearness of his exposition of even the most intricate problems made his lectures stimulating and rewarding. Consequently the college was considered one of the best for the study of electrical engineering.

Dr. Steinmetz was a scientist with a passion for work, uniting the imagination of an artist with a force and intensity that compelled him to make a thorough search into all that was involved in any subject that presented itself to him for observation. Having acquired a command of the English language and the ability to make difficult things easy to understand, he was noted not only as a lecturer but also as a writer for magazines. At meetings of the American Institute of Electrical Engineers, of which he was for some years president, he was usually called upon to close the discussions because of his power of lucid description and explanation, given in forceful and clean-cut phrases.

What did this remarkable man do to benefit in a practical way all the people of America?

For many years engineers had been puzzled over the control of the wonderful electrical forces they had discovered in the rivers and waterfalls. These forces continually broke loose in unaccountable ways, surging along the wires, breaking insulators, and destroying generators and power stations. After a profound study of the problem Dr. Steinmetz devised a method by which the engineers could restrain these forces so that today it is possible to transmit electrical power at high pressure without damage. This is technically called high voltage for power transmission, and it is not unusual now for 200,000 volts to be safely used.

He showed us the possibility of abandoning generating plants of small capacity and furnishing electrical power by substation service from the big trunk supply lines. Much has already been done in this direction in consequence of the work accomplished by Steinmetz.

He greatly benefited all industry by his invention of various motors, such as the induction and polyphase motors. These made possible cheap carlighting and quick elevator service and perfected street lighting. The Steinmetz Law of Magnetism is a method by which engineers can figure how much magnetizing current they should use to magnetize a given piece of iron to be used in an electrical generator or motor, and how hot the iron will become when used in certain conditions. This is considered one of the most valuable things he did.

Dr. Steinmetz was a man of remarkable humility despite his wonderful scientific ability. He invented many other things in addition to the motors mentioned above, particularly a magnetite arc lamp and a mercury arc rectifier. But it was a notable characteristic of his that he was continually giving suggestions to others which assisted them in perfecting their own inventions, thus bringing out the abilities of others. He was so highly regarded, not only by members of his own profession but also by his townsmen, that he held for some years the office of President of the Board of Education of Schenectady and later was made President of the Common Council of that city.

He was very much interested in the National Association of Corporation Schools, of which he became president. The object of this organization was to correlate the educational opportunities of all engaged in industrial work, so that illiteracy and inefficiency might be lessened and production speeded up, and thereby compensation and the standard of living might be raised. He was a Socialist of the kind indicated by the following words of his:

"We must let the big corporations alone . . . [there is] no use in breaking them up into smaller units which cannot be controlled. As soon as the big ones combine under stricter government regulations, the sooner we shall have better working conditions." The benefits conferred by him upon America may well cause Germany to regret that she compelled him to leave his native land.

At his death, which occurred suddenly October 26, 1923, when he was only fifty-eight years of age, appreciation was shown in several ways by the people of the United States. In his home city the public schools were closed the day he died, and flags were at halfmast while his body lay in state. In newspapers and other periodicals his achievements were discussed, and noted scientists paid tribute to "the little cripple with a giant mind." Dr. Steinmetz had proved himself not only a great electrician but a great mathematician. He was an exponent of pure science and applied science also. His service to electrical science was incalculable. From a popular standpoint, his invention of artificial lightning and an "indoor thunderstorm" were of greatest interest. The simplicity of his writings caused some of them to find place in general as well as scientific magazines, and his "Electricity and Civilization," and "Science and Religion" appeared in *Harper's Magazine* the year before his death. He belonged with Millikan, Pupin, and other scientists, who hold that science and religion are not incompatible.

Hideyo Noguchi

IN the northern Aizu district of Honshu, the main island of Japan, stands the magnificent volcanic cone of Bandai. It is inactive now except for a plume of smoke that sometimes leaps from it to stain the blue sky. But twelve hundred years ago it was in eruption, the lava from it destroying whole villages and damming a mountain stream. The backed-up stream formed a beautiful lake, and on its shores, in the shadow of the great mountain, stands the little agricultural village of Okinajima. Its inhabitants are poor. In 1868 they were even poorer, for the Japanese revolution which had overthrown the feudal shoguns, or war lords, had just been concluded. Aizu, a mountain stronghold of feudalism, had held out to the last, and it had been occupied, at great cost, by the soldiers of the Emperor.

Shika Noguchi, whose father was the poorest of the inhabitants of Okinajima, long remembered the occupation, for she and her sickly father had been put out of their house by the soldiers. But Shika remembered something else. She remembered that five generations ago, in the time of Seitaro Noguchi, the house of Noguchi had been a distinguished one. And she prayed to the gods for its restoration. Though she was a poor farm girl in service as a maid in the house of the priest Uno Ura, she accepted his offer to teach her to write. They saved the cost of ink and paper for practicing by sprinkling ashes on a lacquered tray and shaping the ideographs in the ash. The girl learned quickly, and she remembered what she learned, thinking perhaps of her famous ancestors and of the way in which her new-found knowledge might help her to restore her family's dignity.

There was, however, a strong possibility that the Noguchi family would soon be extinct. Shika was the last of the line and, lacking a dowry, she had little hope of winning a husband. But in addition to being a maid with a knowledge of writing, she was a strong girl and a most excellent farmer, far more important considerations in an agricultural community where the women work as hard as the men, standing in the muddy waters of the rice fields from dawn to dusk in winter and in summer. One day Sayosuke the farmer asked her to marry him. Shika agreed, taking the precaution to adopt her future husband first, as is the custom in Japan when one is the last of one's house. Her children would thus bear the Noguchi name. And they would be their mother's children in more than name and birth, for Sayosuke was fond of drinking saki and didn't care for responsibility. When Inu, a girl child, was born, he was disappointed. And when the second child was born, on November 24, 1876, though it was a boy and an occasion for gladness, Shika's husband left her and the two children in the little one-room hut, the only possession which had not yet been sold for saki. Sayosuke went off to live on another island, leaving Shika to care for the children as best she could, only coming back from time to time to beg money from the hard-working girl.

Shika called her son Seisaku, a name which, in conformity with Japanese custom, he would exchange upon reaching maturity, becoming Hideyo Noguchi. "Great-man-of-the-world" is a rough translation of his chosen name, an appellation surely prophetic of his later career. But at the time we are speaking of there was no hint of that great future. Indeed, his mother was so poor that she could not afford to pay anyone a few yen to watch him for her during the day. She had to carry him into the fields with her, depositing him upon a bank while she worked among the rice plants. Later, when his sister Inu was a little older, she left the boy with her. He would sleep close beside the urori, a brazier used for cooking, which provided the only warmth in the little hut. When he awoke, his sister would try to keep the active little three-year-old out of mischief.

One day, however, Shika was longer than usual in

the rice fields. It began to get dark, and Inu, frightened, went to look for her mother. As she walked through the darkening fields, a high-pitched scream from the house she had just left shattered the quietness of the evening. It was followed by another. And another. Turning toward the noise, she saw her mother flash by, tearing savagely at the heavy warazi, the thick clogs to which the sticky mud of the fields clung. Barefooted, Shika raced into the house and snatched her son from the urori, where he was scrambling among the hot coals. Neighbors rushed in.

There was no doctor in the small village, but one of the men examined the boy. "The fingers of the left hand are mostly gone," he said, "and the left arm and the left foot and the right hand are burned, I know not how badly."

The days that followed were terrible ones for Shika. Infection set in, and the little boy almost died. For twenty-one days Shika did not leave her son night or day. She kept her sleepless eyes open by wedging bits of wood between the lids. And as she nursed the boy back to health, she gradually straightened the crumpled fingers of the right hand, manipulating them until they gained strength. For the left hand she could do nothing. It remained a crooked stump with a few knob-like protrusions where the fingers had been.

Gradually Seisaku recovered. Hereafter, his mother would take him with her wherever she went, hanging the basket in which he slept in a tree while she worked, or letting him romp in the fields nearby where she could watch him. As he grew, Shika kept him close to her, teaching him what she had learned in the household of the priest. By the time he was ready for school, he was already far in advance of his classmates. Jealous of his learning, they began to taunt him, shouting "Tembo, tembo," or "hand boy," in mockery of his deformed hand. Angered by their taunts, the boy withdrew to his books, studying harder when he realized that he could never become a good farmer with his misshapen hand.

However, the cost of attending school was a severe drain, and young Seisaku had to work to keep himself there. Mornings he would fish in Lake Inawashiro, selling his catch in the town before going to class. After school he carried baggage, often traveling as far as ten miles with a heavy burden through winter snows. At night he tended the wood fire that heated the water in the communal bath house. He got no money for this latter job, but he was allowed to read in the light of the fire. At home he could not read after the sun went down because it was always dark there, the family being too poor to buy fuel for such purposes.

Through the assistance of Sakae Kobayashi, a kindly school principal from Inawashiro who recognized his ability, Seisaku was able to enter the kotto-shogakko, the Japanese secondary school. There he soon excelled even his teachers in such subjects as drawing, science, and English, and he was at the head of the class in all of his subjects. Finishing his own work rapidly, he would help his fellow students with theirs. He would help, that is, if they pretended to ignore his deformed left hand, which he was extremely sensitive about and tried to conceal, drawing it up into the wide sleeve of his kimono. But Kobayashi-san had seen the useless hand and he thought that something might be done for it by a skillful doctor. Taking up a collection among the fathers of the boys in the kotto-shogakko, he sent young Seisaku off to Wakamatsu one wonderful day with money to see a doctor he had heard of in that city.

Seisaku walked the twenty miles to Wakamatsu with rising hope in his heart. There he saw the strange doctor who had been educated abroad and who wore trousers and a waistcoat instead of the traditional kimono. Kanae Watanabe was his name, and after examining the boy's hand carefully, he told him that much could be done for it. He wished to operate immediately. Would Seisaku like something to deaden the pain? The boy shook his head. "But if you have a book, let me read it meanwhile," he said.

Many treatments followed the initial operation, Seisaku walking the twenty miles to be treated and twenty miles back home. But Watanabe-san was a great doctor, and he worked miracles with the hand. He could not, of course, restore the fingers. But he separated the stumps, enabling each to move independently and perform useful functions. And the scar tissue that had drawn the hand to the wrist was severed, allowing the hand to hang naturally. Seisaku had, in effect, a new hand. And he had a new aim as well. He was determined to be a doctor.

Talking with the doctor while he was being treated, Seisaku gave voice to his ambition. Since the doctor needed another boy in his house to run errands, mix medicines, and help with patients, Seisaku was apprenticed to him at once. He would learn what he could through observation. He would also have access to the doctor's library, which included many works in English, German, and French, as well as medical texts in Japanese. Seisaku knew no German or French, but he soon took advantage of the opportunities of this relatively large city to find someone who would teach him those languages. And so that he might have more time for studying, he cut his sleeping time down to three hours a night, imitating Napoleon, whom he read about in one of Dr. Watanabe's books.

With the outbreak of the first Sino-Japanese war Dr. Watanabe, an ex-military surgeon, left for the front, leaving young Seisaku in charge of his domestic affairs. When he returned in 1894, he was delighted to find his household account books in perfect order and his affairs running smoothly. He was overwhelmed when he discovered that the boy, studying by himself, had quite prepared himself for the first examinations at the Tokyo Medical School. The passing of these examinations admitted him to the school with advanced standing, and he entered the institution later that year with financial help from Dr. Watanabe and his old friend and teacher Kobayashi-san.

In Tokyo Seisaku lived on next to nothing. Dr. Chiwaki, a friend whom he had met at Dr. Watanabe's home, worked in the Takagama Dental College there, and he got Seisaku a job ringing the class bell and polishing the school lamps. When Seisaku lost his job because he became interested in a book and forgot to ring the bell signifying the end of class, Dr. Chiwaki contributed fifteen yen a month to the boy's support. In this way Seisaku continued at the Medical College. A poor one by modern standards and frowned upon even in those days by graduates of the Imperial University, the college offered little beyond a rather uninspired series of lectures. But Seisaku stuck it out for three years, graduating in 1897. Passing the government examination, he became a licensed physican and surgeon.

Hideyo, as young Noguchi began to call himself about this time, did not go into practice as a physician upon being licensed. Ever since the day he had first looked through a microscope in the house of Dr.

Watanabe, he had wanted to be a bacteriologist and study the minute organisms that he had observed beneath the lens. But before he could undertake independent research, much more study would be necessary. He would have to go abroad, to America and to Germany, where the great men of science had their laboratories. Meanwhile, he worked at the Jutendo General Hospital, editing a medical journal. Also, through the aid of Dr. Chiwaki, he became a lecturer in general pathology and oral surgery at the Tokyo Dental College. Soon, however, he had an opportunity to follow his inclination for research work, and he joined the staff of Dr. Kitasato at the Government Institute of Infectious Diseases. He was even promised that he would be able to study abroad under government sponsorship. But he would have to wait five years for that.

In the meantime, bubonic plague had broken out in China, and Noguchi was sent to New Chwang under the auspices of the International Sanitary Board. He was made physician-in-chief to the Central Medical Bureau, comprising both a hospital and a bacteriological laboratory. Later, the plague having disappeared from the region, he was transferred to Manchuria under a Russian medical commission, where he remained until the Boxer Rebellion. Then he returned to Tokyo, busying himself with the publication of several books, including texts on the methods of pathological and bacteriological study and the translation of a German manual of hygiene.

One day while Noguchi was at work at the institute, several American scientists came to visit Dr. Kitasato, who enjoyed an international reputation for his work on diphtheria immunization. Among them was Dr. Simon Flexner, who was returning to America and a new job at the University of Pennsylvania. Noguchi talked with the man, expressing his desire to visit America for study. Despite the fact that, according to Dr. Flexner, "no particular encouragement was given to this request," Noguchi appeared on the University of Pennsylvania campus the following year, having borrowed 300 yen from his friend Chiwaki to make the trip. He had little money left when he arrived, and there was, of course, no job at the university for the unexpected visitor. But Dr. Flexner did his best for the young Oriental, introducing him to Dr. Silas Weir Mitchell. A man already famous for his work on snake venoms, Dr. Mitchell interested Noguchi in the subject, providing him with funds sufficient to cover the cost of his experiments and a modest sum for living expenses. Noguchi was soon writing confidently to friends in Japan, "I have entered the sweet realm of science."

Having less that $25 a month during his first year in America, Noguchi lived precariously. But his work on the venoms progressed rapidly and, as he expressed it, "except for eating and drinking there is only experimentation." Soon his work was being recognized as important in scientific circles. Dr. Mitchell interested the National Academy of Science in it, and a contribution from the Bache Fund was made to extend the scope of investigation. Later the Carnegie Institute granted funds to the young Japanese scientist. As various aspects of the study were completed, Noguchi published the results in the University of Pennsylvania Medical Bulletin and in other scientific periodicals. Eventually the results of the studies as a whole were brought together in a handsome, illustrated volume published by the Carnegie Institute. But before that happened, Noguchi was given his long-hoped-for opportunity to study in Europe. Receiving a Carnegie fellowship for a year's study abroad, he went to Copenhagen, Denmark, to work under Thorwald Madsen at the Staatens Serum Institut. And when he returned to America, in 1904, a position was awaiting him in the newly opened Rockefeller Institute for Medical Research in New York. Writing home at the beginning of his fifth year away from Japan, Noguchi said, "In fact I will stay in America for a long time. The reason is that it has much more future at every point than Japan."

At the Rockefeller Institute Noguchi worked on a number of problems. He worked on trachoma, a serious eye disease, but temporarily turned from "this rather resultless subject." He published some further observations on venom—the list of his articles had grown to twenty by now. He investigated tetanus. Then he turned to the problem of blood serum. Next he tackled the dread disease syphilis, developing a modification of the famed Wassermann test, and discovering a method of diagnosing *tabes dorsalis,* a form of paralysis caused by the disease, by tapping the spinal fluid. His book on the diagnosis of syphilis followed.

Then, in October of 1910, Noguchi brought one of his most significant pieces of work at the Institute to a triumphant conclusion and thus attracted worldwide attention. That scientific feat was the cultivation of the Spirochaeta pallida, the pale spirochete assumed to be the cause of syphilis. The organism had first been seen by Schaudinn in 1905, but no one had been able to cultivate it by itself, to grow it unmixed with other organisms in what is called a pure culture. Until someone produced the disease in an animal with a pure culture, it could not be determined whether some other organism—unknown, unseen, perhaps unseeable—was not the true cause of the disease. Noguchi solved the riddle by producing the pale spirochete for the first time and infecting a laboratory animal from his culture. From the culture he also developed a product called luetin, of use in detecting latent and congenital syphilis.

Valuable as the specific discovery was, its significance was small compared with the consequence issuing from it, namely, the perfection of a method for the pure cultivation of the class of spirochetal microorganisms. Noguchi now cultivated a horde of spirochetes that no one had been able to cultivate before, including among many others the spirochetes of European and African relapsing fevers. Mastering the field of spirochetes, he turned to other fields, isolating the granular bodies causing trachoma, an eye disease which he had once studied and given up as "resultless."

Then he turned to a still different problem—and a big one. Working on a hunch that general paralysis of the insane is syphilis of the brain, he sought the spirochete of syphilis in the brains of dead paretics, perfecting new microscopic methods of examining the diseased tissue. And he found what he was seeking both in the brain tissues of those who had died of general paralysis and in the spinal cords of victims of locomotor ataxia, thereby linking those two common and terrible diseases and establishing their cause.

Hideyo Noguchi was by now universally recognized as a great man of the world of science. The University of Pennsylvania granted him an honorary degree. He was made a full member of the Rockefeller Institute, along with Dr. Carrel, Professor Loeb, and his former teacher, Dr. Flexner. Offered the presidency of the Peru Research Institute and the directorship of the Agriculture Department of Great Britain, he declined these offers and the large salaries that went with them, preferring to remain in America. His wife, the former Mary Dardis, was an American, and, though prejudicial naturalization laws prevented him from becoming an American citizen, he had adopted her country since his marriage in 1912. He did, however, accept the invitation to lecture before the Versammlung deutscher Naturforscher und Aertze in Vienna. To lecture before those Germans whom he had always considered the great men of science! And when he went abroad, his trip through Europe was a triumphal one. He was recognized and deferred to everywhere. And he was similarly acclaimed on his trip to Japan in 1915, where he was awarded the Imperial Prize of the Japanese Academy.

But fame, that last infirmity of noble minds, was no longer a spur to him. He had long ago asserted his independence of its promptings in a letter written, in his curiously poetic English, to a friend in Japan:

Since I came to this country I have learned besides science something of the ends of life, something about withering and blooming, what they mean . . . In this whirlpool of confusion we should keep hope and virtue. If you realize these two it will be happiness. I have already realized one half of my purpose in coming to America and the other half is fate and work. If I confess my ideal when I came it was narrow and small. It was largely, no, it was entirely to get glory. That was first with me. But this thinking has been destroyed and now I want to consecrate my life to one great task.

His life had become completely consecrated to scientific research. After his lecture tours he was eager to get back to his work, for his mind had lain fallow long enough. He returned to America to investigate the fatal Rocky Mountain spotted fever, discovering a serum that would suppress the infection. He settled the question of the relationship between two obscure South American diseases, oroya fever and *verruga peruana,* establishing them as variants of carrion's disease and forwarding work on its carriers. He cultivated the "globoid bodies" from the virus disease poliomyelitis, advancing research in that field. And from 1918, when he became a member of the Rockefeller Foundation Commission sent to Ecuador, until his death in 1928, he worked intermittently on yellow fever. Indeed, it was of that disease that he died in South Africa, like Adrian Stokes, whose conclusions about the disease his own investigations supported. And those conclusions were destructive of his own widely accepted earlier hypothesis about the cause of the disease!

Leading a dedicated life, Hideyo Noguchi was something more than a great scientist. He was a great man as well. He was correct in saying that he had learned "besides science something of the ends of life, something about withering and blooming . . ."

Probably without this knowledge no man is ever great. Without it no man can be anything more than a skillful machine. And with it . . . ?

With it there are men like Noguchi, who would play chess with a friend until two o'clock in the morning and then go back to the laboratory to work through the remainder of the night. With it Noguchi would master languages—English, French, German, Chinese, Danish, Italian, Spanish, Russian—with the same intensity he displayed in mastering knowledge of species of bacteria. He would paint forcefully or fish wildly in the little stream behind his summer cottage in the Catskills. Then he would turn with equal passion to his test tubes. He would listen to his wife reading the *Kreutzer Sonata* to him while he examined slides bearing diseased tissue from the human brain. He would find the book abominable and be able to say why. And in the two-hundredth slide he would find the cause of a fatal disease, a spiral bacteria which no one else had been able to locate.

If Noguchi's ideal was "narrow and small" when he first came to America, certainly it grew enormously while he was here. As he said, he learned something of the ends of life. And, having learned, perhaps he was still able to say, as he watched the progress in his own body of the disease he had observed so often in others, "There is some good fate in how my affairs are, and my research is entering a sweet realm."

Angelo Patri

Today thousands of children and parents alike rejoice in the fact that Angelo Patri left Italy to become a teacher in America, because he helped to make learning interesting for children and was largely responsible for bringing about a community spirit that was enormously beneficial to parents, teachers, and children.

He was born in Italy in November, 1877. He still remembers how, evening after evening, in the old country, his father would tell stories of the knights of the crusades or the heroes of Italy, entertaining the children and inspiring them with the love of the great and the good. He also remembers the journey to America, where his family settled in a happy colony of fellow countrymen in New York's Little Italy.

At the age of eleven Angelo began to attend school in his new country, but the monotony of it wearied the little foreign boy. The teacher would write the lesson on the board, and the children were compelled to recite it after her. Day after day, year after year, the method never varied. Angelo had always been a nervous child, and he endured agonies when he was forced, under rigid school discipline, to sit without moving and listen to the dull, unending drone of the lessons. It was only through a great effort of will that he forced himself to conform to the harsh ways of the school.

His home life had changed, too. There were no more stories of knights in shining armor, for his father always returned from work too exhausted to spin tales for the children. Furthermore, the boy was constantly busy preparing his dull lessons for uninspired repetition on the following day. Soon the family had to move away from their friends in Little Italy, and they lost themselves in the big, busy American city. It seemed to little Angelo as though gradually all friendly human relations were being replaced by mechanical routines. Yet his father, with a poet's soul, helped to nourish the boy's soul, too. He inspired in his son respect for the mind and the spirit. And when the right time came, he encouraged the boy to go to college, hoping that he would eventually enter the priesthood.

Young Angelo attended the College of the City of New York, where he studied hard in the hope of fulfilling his father's wishes by entering a seminary upon graduating. But these dreams were not to be realized, at least, not in the way he had anticipated. One day while Angelo was still at college, his father fell fifty feet from a ladder on which he had been working. He did not recover from the accident for a whole year, so Angelo gave up the idea of becoming a priest. With his father unable to earn money, he had to find work. Therefore, as soon as his degree was conferred, in 1897, he sought a job as a teacher in the New York city school system.

As a beginning teacher Angelo was told to emphasize discipline. He dutifully carried out his severe instructions, banging knuckles, tugging hair, and bullying for all he was worth. His students learned little and disliked him intensely, but they sat up straight and kept quiet. Since school boards were interested in little else in those days, Angelo, with a reputation for efficiency, was promoted to a fifth-year class. But here his methods of obtaining discipline proved ineffectual, for the older students defied him. Forced to take a different tack, he remembered the stories he had heard his father tell in his own childhood, and he began to repeat them. His classes listened attentively, and when they were informed that their efforts would be rewarded with more stories, they worked hard.

After teaching for a year Angelo Patri discovered that he had become the slave of a system, following a prescribed syllabus that never varied. The course of study failed to make provision for the individual differences of students, and it did not allow the

teacher to take advantage of thought-provoking situations as they arose. Patri saw in his work nothing
but a "deadly mechanical grind," and after another
year he decided to seek a remedy for the situation. He
found such a remedy in *Ethical Principles*, the book
of the great American philosopher, John Dewey. This
book taught him that conduct was the real test of
learning, that the teacher must watch and guide but
could not force. He must not attempt to force his
own arbitrary mold on the child's developing personality. Instead he must seek to draw out the child,
guiding him, of course, but guiding him along paths
determined by his own character. This method
should be the inspiration of the teacher. Unfortunately, when Angelo Patri tried to put his new concepts into practice he was stymied by old-fashioned
supervisors, and he was forced to change schools. Ul-
timately he found a principal whose motto, "To
serve the children," was in harmony with his own
new-found tenets.

In 1908 Patri was himself appointed principal of
a school, Public School No. 4 in the Bronx of New
York city. He was the first Italian-born American to
be appointed a school principal in the United States,
and he served with distinction in this capacity from
1908 until 1913.

But there was another school in the Bronx more
badly in need of his expert guidance: Public School

No. 45. And in 1913 Principal Patri was transferred to that difficult school. At first he met with nothing but discouragement, for the teachers, not understanding his ideas, feared him and his new methods. He had to work hard to convince them of his sincerity, taking their problem students and personally dealing with them. Gradually he won their respect and with it the respect of the students. Treated like human beings, problem students responded. They were given jobs to do which made them responsible members of the school community. School pride began to replace fear as a motivating force in Principal Angelo Patri's school.

But another problem troubled Patri. As a principal he had not only to contend with problem children and unsympathetic teachers but with upset parents as well. Parents often misunderstood the motives of the school in dealing with their children. Patri tried to explain his policies. Slowly, he brought the neighboring people into touch with the school. One man came to see the principal in great excitement, explaining that his sons, going home in peaceable fashion, had been attacked by a gang. Patri investigated and reported his findings to the father, who was much surprised to learn that his second son had confessed to being one of the gang leaders. Realizing the seriousness of the matter, the father pitched in to help the principal get some after-school activities started for the children. They visited a real estate dealer on the corner of the school street and talked him into allowing the children to use a nearby vacant lot for making a garden. He also allowed them to use an empty room in the rear of his office for storing their tools. Many of the boys were soon busy hoeing corn and picking tomatoes. Gang warfare subsided.

A mother came to complain to Patri about a truant schoolgirl who had taken her baby from its carriage in front of the house and abandoned it a few blocks away. Patri sent for the girl's mother and learned that she could not properly supervise her daughter because she had to care for a crippled husband. Hearing this story, the mother whose baby had been abducted volunteered to bring the offending girl to school every day. She did so for almost a year, until the child was in the habit of arriving regularly without her. By then, however, the self-appointed truant officer had acquired a real interest in the school, and she continued to participate in its activities.

Incidents such as these made Angelo Patri feel that he was succeeding with the parents as well as with the children. He discovered, too, that the teachers were becoming more intimate and friendly with the parents, and that was another step in the right direction. This intimacy he fostered by sponsoring entertainments in which the children took part. Eventually, a Parents' Association was formed for the purpose of discussing and acting upon parent-teacher problems.

The next step for the benefit of the community was the acquisition of an after-school clubhouse for the children. An old house was obtained and converted to that use. Each month ten thousand children went in and out of this building to attend their music, drawing, sewing, civic, athletic, and literary clubs. A playground adjoined the building and a dispensary was opened where free medical attention was provided by a doctor and his wife who had become interested in the project. The president of the Parents' Association formed a church committee which secured property and began to erect a new school building for which church people furnished the funds. A home visitor was obtained to investigate problems growing out of difficult home conditions. The woman who undertook this job was known as Aunt Margaret, and her sympathetic understanding enabled her to accomplish a great deal in this important sphere.

Mr. Patri abandoned the dull, old-fashioned school assembly. Instead he dramatized folk tales and introduced the songs and dances of the various national groups whose members sent their children to his school. He encouraged the children to take home to their parents what they learned and suggested that the parents tell them their own folk tales. He also started making Arbor Day a great annual festival.

On that day each year some three thousand children with their mothers, aunts, and cousins gathered before the school doors were opened. The day was begun by a play given in the assembly hall, and that was followed by the planting of trees furnished by the park department. In the afternoon games and dances were conducted for the whole community.

Experience taught Dr. Patri the wisdom of assigning a troublesome child to a teacher whom the child liked. Often the relationship thus formed lasted throughout the school life of the child and beyond it. Children who were too fast or too slow for the work of the regular schoolroom were given special assignments under sympathetic and understanding direction. Carpentry and reed and raffia work were introduced, and trained instructors were employed to direct these craft lessons. An outlet was thus provided for talents not formerly appreciated in the schools.

Children whose work was below standard were examined carefully for physical defects which might be handicapping them; poor eyesight, trouble with tonsils, adenoids, bad teeth or indigestion could then be remedied. Though all this care involved extra work, Patri undertook it in the spirit of service, considering it the duty of the schools to help the pupils become useful members of society.

The idea toward which Patri worked was that life and school must become one. The first step must be sound: the child's personality must not be suppressed by a method which forced him to conform to a meaningless routine for purposes of economy. Patri objected to such false economy, insisting, "We need the scientist, the artist, the specialist in the first year of school." He ridiculed the idea of putting "fifty children under one teacher, thinking we cannot afford anything better. . . ." Unfortunately, his efforts in this direction have been least successful, and educational budgets still remain inadequate.

Teachers who had been trained under the old system, which insisted that the teacher be a taskmaster setting arbitrary exercises and sternly overseeing their execution, were required to re-examine each task and question each purpose. The teacher, Patri said, must continually ask, "What is the effect of my program on the soul growth of the children?" He insisted that, in order to accomplish his purpose, a teacher must know the child and his potentialities. To know the child, to work so that he may grow, is a far bigger thing than anything else in the world. And this, Patri said, is the difficult job of every single teacher.

Angelo Patri never became a priest, as his father had wished. But his devotion to his job from the beginning was priest-like, and he provided inspiration for thousands of teachers, parents, and pupils. He has become widely known through his articles on education that are syndicated in many newspapers. He has also written several books, the best known being *A Schoolmaster in a Great City* (1917), *Child Training* (1922), *The Spirit of America* (1928), and *The Questioning Child* (1931). *The Spirit of America,* a civics textbook, is particularly interesting as a reflection upon American institutions by a foreign-born citizen who has helped to improve them so greatly.

Albert Einstein

A GERMAN Jew—Albert Einstein, a theoretic physicist, one of the greatest thinkers of all time and one of the greatest geniuses of the modern world —became an American citizen in 1940, and the United States may well be proud of this searcher after truth. Experiments and measurements he always left to other physicists, while he observed, imagined, *thought*. And his thought has caused a revolution in scientific ideas.

When he was a very little boy, Albert was thought by his parents to be mentally deficient because his mental processes seemed backward and the power of speech came slowly. They seem to have been ordinary townspeople to whom the child was born in 1879 at Ulm, Germany. A year later the family moved to Munich. The father carried on an electrical business and was interested in engineering. He was of a kindly, optimistic nature, but he never made a great success. He had renounced the Jewish faith and was a materialist in thought. The mother, more serious in some ways but with a sense of humor, was a lover of people and devoted to her family. The only apparent likeness between mother and son was a love of music. At six years of age Albert played the violin and at twelve had a passion for music beyond his years, playing mostly Mozart, Beethoven, and Bach. This love stayed with him throughout his life and was always his solace and recreation.

The schools of Munich had little educational ideal; they were crude, severe, and compulsory in method, and as a boy Albert Einstein hated classes. He felt alone with an "inner loneliness"; he found little sympathy at home, and in school he had a feeling of isolation and did not associate with his schoolmates. Dr. Max Talmy writes that he felt it his good fortune to come in contact with this boy who was then ten years old. For five years they were intimate friends. He gave Albert a book on physics and his first book on mathematics. He comments: "When Albert was about thirteen the flight of his mathematical genius was so high and swift I could no longer follow him." They turned to philosophy, and Kant, incomprehensible to many adults, "seemed clear to this young schoolboy." His first geometry excited him, and he went on eagerly to other branches of mathematics. He never excelled in languages or in anything that called for memorizing. But now his teachers recognized his ability, and he was considered a genius. For years he had felt a growing love of nature; in his long lone walks its wonders and its beauties had developed a true reverence in him. As a little child Albert showed a religious interest, largely due to this association with nature. He is reported to have composed little songs of praise to God and to have sung them at home and on the street. In early adolescence his religious feeling was related to music and other forms of art in which he had an increasing interest. Later, other interests supplanted that of religion, except that in adult life it expressed itself in what Dr. Einstein termed cosmic religion.

When he was sixteen years of age his father's business failed. The family decided to venture anew in Milan, Italy. This led to a great and delightful change for young Einstein. He was allowed six months' freedom from schooling and spent his time in art museums, in reading, and in seeing the natural beauties of Italy, which he loved. He lived in a dream and was little fitted for ordinary pursuits. His chief desire was to be free. He renounced his German citizenship and cared little for his Jewish heritage. Finally, he was sent to Switzerland to take entrance examinations at Zurich Academy. In these he failed, and necessity forced him to go to a lower school. In its liberal atmosphere he was happy, and in a year's time he was enabled to enter the Academy.

For some time there had been growing a great change in his mental interest and attitude. He became indifferent to mathematics and turned to philosophy rather than science, except for his devotion to physics. He read with avidity the works of the great physicists and at this period sought empirical methods for the solution of problems. He showed an intellectual hunger for knowledge, but the methods of the lecture room bored him, and he cut many of his classes, though the college had some famous teachers. Einstein lived in solitude on a small income and often was undernourished. A few kindred spirits became his friends: Marcel Grossman, an able woman who studied with him and years later assisted him in working out his theories; the Austrian socialist, Friedrich Adler, who was a physicist and seemed to Einstein a pure idealist. He read also with Mileva Maric, a Serbian, who afterward became his first wife. In later life he married a widowed cousin, Elsa, with whom he had played in childhood. She died in 1936.

Upon graduation, Einstein's father planned for him to seek an engineering position. This was abhorrent to the son. It was, however, necessary for him to earn his living. After attempts at tutoring in a struggle to earn enough to keep himself alive, he felt more keenly the injustices of life which he had observed as a child. He had noted then the unjust discrimination against the poor. Now he felt it personally. At the age of twenty-three he obtained a position at the Patent Office of Berne. This work required insight and judgment, and he liked it; also it allowed opportunity to pursue his investigations in physics. While there Einstein developed and published his theory of relativity in its restricted form— the remarkable achievement of a scientific imagination. In his excitement over this and other discoveries in physics he exclaimed, "It was as if a storm had broken loose in my head!" During this time he took his Ph.D. from Zurich University. And while at Berne he married, and a son was born to him. His life satisfied him now, and he was content to remain where he was. In his student days he had become a citizen of Switzerland. By 1909, however, Einstein's writings were known, and through the influence of one of his old professors he was appointed extraordinary professor of theoretic physics at the University of Zurich. He was invited to lecture in several European cities, then accepted the chair of physics at Prague University in 1911. Two years later Professor Einstein was urged to return to Zurich, this time to a full professorship in his old Polytechnic Academy. From there he went to Berlin. His ability was so generally recognized that a special position was created for him as director of the Kaiser Wilhelm Physical Institute. He was elected a member of the Royal Prussian Academy of Sciences and received an income sufficient to allow him to devote much time to research.

In 1915 Dr. Einstein put forth his *General Theory of Relativity,* and at the celebration of his fiftieth anniversary, Professor A. A. Michelson, a world-famous scientist, said, "Dr. Einstein's theory of relativity has caused a revolution in scientific thought unprecedented in the history of science." In his modest, unobtrusive way, Einstein turned to Michelson, saying, "It was you who led the physicists into new paths, and through your marvelous experimental work paved the way for the development of the theory of relativity; it was your verifications which first set the theory on a real basis." Robert Millikan on this occasion said, "You can throw general relativity into the wastebasket if you will, and Professor Einstein's position as the leading mind in the development of our modern physics would still remain unchallenged." This was said in a leading magazine fifteen years later: "The main achievement of the general theory of relativity is that it has advanced a uniformity of view of the physical world structure."

In an interesting article (*Forum,* October, 1930) entitled "What I Believe," Dr. Einstein said:

Many times a day I realize how much my own outer and inner life is built upon the labors of my fellow men both living and dead, and how earnestly I must exert myself in order to give in return as much as I have received. My peace of mind is often troubled by the depressing sense that I have borrowed too heavily from

the work of other men. . . . Without the sense of col-
laborating with like-minded beings in the pursuit of
the ever unattainable in art and scientific research,
my life would have been empty.

Yet Dr. Einstein loved solitude and cared little for
ordinary social contacts, saying of himself, "My pas-
sionate interest in social justice and social responsibility has always stood in curious contrast to a marked
lack of desire for direct association with men and
women. I am a horse for single harness, not cut out
for tandem or team work."

Like some other geniuses, he was careless as to ap-
pearances. He hated publicity too. When newspaper
men and crowds of people assembled to greet him on
arrival in America, he tried to get away, saying in his
shy, embarrassed manner, "*Why* do they do it?" He
had a soft voice and kindly eye and smile but sometimes grew irate under annoyance and interruption.
Humility, sincerity, and integrity were his striking
characteristics. Popular estimation must be due more
to his personality than to his scientific eminence. It
has been said, "No one can meet Professor Einstein
for the first time without an immediate realization
of extraordinary intellectual power combined with a
natural simplicity and kindliness which so often char-
acterizes great genius."

The honors conferred upon Dr. Einstein were
many. The leading universities of Europe gave him

degrees, and several scientific academies elected him to membership. In 1921 he was awarded the Nobel prize; the Copley medal of the Royal Society was presented to him in 1925; and in 1926 the Royal Astronomical Society of London bestowed on him its highest distinction, the gold medal. He expressed his gratitude to this Society in these words:

> The man who has discovered an idea which allows us to penetrate, to whatever slight degree, a little more deeply the eternal mystery of nature has been allotted a great share of grace. If, in addition, he experiences the best help, sympathy and recognition of his time, he attains almost more happiness than one man can bear.

Help, sympathy, and recognition were not forthcoming from all quarters, however. Dr. Einstein's happiness was leavened with rage and woe when the Nazis came to power in Germany. Hitler and his brutal minions were incapable of sympathy and respect, and they helped only themselves. One of the things they helped themselves to was a sum of money that Albert Einstein had on deposit in Germany. Their justification for this theft—confiscation, they called it—was that Einstein was a Jew and an intellectual. Intellectuals, furthering thought, were suspect by the propaganda mongers of the police state. And Jews were condemned because they worshiped God rather than the state.

The Nazis were particularly vicious in their treatment of Jews. Their outrages caused Dr. Einstein to identify himself more closely with the Jewish people. Eagerly assisting the Jews in every way possible, he encouraged them to help themselves through peaceful self-assertion as a national unit among the nations of the world. A strong believer in Zionism, he was an influential supporter of the movement which resulted in the establishment of a Jewish nation in Palestine.

The greatest thinker of our time, Dr. Einstein actively fostered free thought. He helped to establish and carry on the Hebrew University in Jerusalem, expressing the hope that "our University will always be free from a spirit of narrow nationalism, that teachers and students will always preserve the consciousness that they serve their people best when they maintain its union with humanity and with the highest human values." In America, too, Dr. Einstein spoke out against the narrow nationalism that would destroy our freedom while loudly proclaiming its glories.

From childhood Einstein had a horror of war and all that is involved in it. He called himself a militant pacifist. He despised war and had a contempt for the man who marches to music to kill another. "I would rather," he said, "be smitten to shreds than participate in such doings." His political ideal was democracy, and during his later years he made his home in Princeton, New Jersey, where he was a member of The Institute for Advanced Study.

When he was asked some years ago for a formula for success in life he replied, "If A is success in life, I should say the formula is $A = X + Y + Z$, X being work and Y being play." "And what is Z?" he was asked. "That," he answered, "is keeping your mouth shut."

Dr. Einstein's religious views were indicative of the man. He said:

Everything that men do or think concerns the satisfaction of the needs they feel, or the escape from pain. This must be kept in mind when we seek to understand spiritual or intellectual movements and the way in which they develop. For feeling and longing are the motive forces of all human striving and productivity —however nobly these latter may display themselves to us. What then are the feelings and the needs which have brought mankind to religious thought and to faith in the widest sense? A moment's consideration shows that the most varied emotions stand at the cradle of religious thought and experience. In primitive peoples it is, first of all, fear that awakens religious ideas —fear of hunger, of wild animals, of illness and of death. A second source of religious development is found in the social feelings. The longing for guidance, for love and succor, provides the stimulus for the growth of a social or moral conception of God. This is the God of Providence who protects, decides, rewards and punishes. . . . This is the social or moral idea of God. Only exceptionally gifted individuals or especially noble communities rise essentially above this level; in these there is found a third level of religious experience. I will call it the cosmic religious sense. This is hard to make clear to those who do not experience it, since it does not involve an anthropomorphic idea of God; the individual feels the vanity of human desires and aims, and the nobility and marvelous order which are revealed in nature and in the world of thought.

Again he said:

The most beautiful thing we can experience is the mysterious. It is the source of all true art and science. He to whom this emotion is a stranger, who can no longer pause to wonder and stand rapt in awe, is as good as dead: his eyes are closed. This insight into the mystery of life, coupled though it be with fear, has also given rise to religion. To know that what is impenetrable to us really exists, manifesting itself as the highest wisdom and the most radiant beauty which our dull faculties can comprehend only in their most primitive forms—this knowledge, this feeling, is at the center of true religiousness. In this sense and in this sense only, I belong in the ranks of devoutly religious men.

Dr. Einstein died at the age of seventy-six, on April 18, 1955.

Hendrik Willem van Loon

ISTORIAN, journalist, artist and educator—all
these terms have been applied to Hendrik Willem van Loon, an evidence of his versatile character
and ability. His life was a varied one, travel and other
influences having contributed as much to his education as schools. A Dutchman, he spent his first twenty-
one years in his native land. The last forty-one years
he was an American, remembering always his origin
in Holland. Born in old Rotterdam in 1882, the son
of Hendrik Willem and Elizabeth Johanna, he re-
tained the simplicity, sincerity and heartiness of the
Dutch. His father, whom he remembered as a sour,
unhappy man who was unkind to children, contributed nothing to Hendrik's zest for life. Perhaps it
was by way of contrast that the son learned the value
of fun, for he considered an appreciation of joy a
great need in life. And he carried his sense of humor
into the delightful books that he wrote for children.

Hendrik Willem's early education was a sad one
both at home and in the private schools of Holland.
In an article entitled *How Not to Educate Children*

he revealed the weaknesses, as he saw them, of the present-day system of education and, at the same time, from personal experience showed the terrible requirements of the old system gone forever—except in memory. "There is not one single agreeable memory connected with my childhood," said he, and he grew up with a "bitter hatred" for his own youth, so much so that, as a man, he added, "The Kingdom of the Netherlands of forty years ago was a veritable Hell for children." In referring to his father's cruelty he told how he could never forget "the day when I had made myself a replica of de Ruyter's flagship and heard it slowly being squashed to pieces beneath the heavy heels of the author of my being." When a grandfather invited children and grandchildren to go to a circus and they were all ready to go, the grandchildren were sent back to school and made to write an essay on "The Moral Advantage of Disappointments." In boarding school the pupils were obliged to study from seven in the morning till eleven at night.

On coming to this country van Loon studied at Cornell and Harvard universities. Later he returned to Europe and took his doctorate from the University of Munich. Previous to the gaining of his doctorate, van Loon turned to journalism. He was Associated Press correspondent in Washington and at Moscow, St. Petersburg, and Warsaw during the Revolution in Russia. After his period of study at Munich he returned to this country and lectured on history and the history of art at several universities in the United States.

When war broke out in Europe in 1914 van Loon again went as Associated Press correspondent, this time to Belgium; later and until the end of the war he was correspondent in a number of European countries. For a year he had a lectureship in modern European history at Cornell University. In 1922 he became Professor of History at Antioch College, Ohio. But a year later he turned again to journalism, becoming associate editor of the Baltimore *Sun*. Some years afterward he was traveling and lecturing in Australia, New Zealand, South Africa, and South America. In looking back on his experiences Dr. van Loon said: "I have spent some three years of my life on the high seas, and I have been in a great many parts of the world, and I have crossed the ocean in everything from a fifty-thousand-ton liner to a one-ton lifeboat." When writing of the value of travel he said that "for those who travel with their heads even a very short trip of only a few hours will bring more enlightenment than any number of learned articles."

After seeing many places his native land must have had charm for him, for he made a home on the Island of Veere, Holland. There he and his wife lived in rustic simplicity. Surrounded by books, maps and many unique drawings, he would develop his work and

Mrs. van Loon would assist in preparation for the publishers. Visitors often received cordial welcome from the van Loons at Veere and at their equally unpretentious home in Connecticut. A story is told of an impromptu visit when the host himself cooked fried eggs from a "secret recipe" and served them with much gusto. The walls of the study and living room at Veere were decorated with maps and sketches of ships and little Dutch villages. On one wall in the study was painted by his own hand a panoramic picture of *The Story of Mankind*, from the fishes in the sea to the towering skyscrapers of modern days. In the living room another showed a gay map of many colors and figures representing the world. His home in Old Greenwich, Connecticut, was as colorful and hospitable as the attractive house he made famous in Veere.

For many years Dr. van Loon devoted himself to writing and illustrating his own books. He was a prolific writer, and his articles were in many of the magazines. Most of his works are voluminous but chatty, being woven of many interesting details. Tales, anecdotes, and word-pictures that at first sight might seem to be digressions are really illustrative of the subject in hand. He knew his facts and could make them live. In all there is a style peculiarly the author's own which leads one to recognize one of his books by familiarity with others.

One of the earliest books is *The Story of Mankind* and here we find many interesting facts in a small space. Beginning with prehistoric man we go on to a short story of Egypt, Mesopotamia, and the Indo-Europeans. Then we go to Greece and Rome and on to Western Europe, where we see modern society developing. Finally, we come to the history of later centuries, crowded with discoveries, new developments and inventions. The author's pen-and-ink drawings add interest and in most instances enlightenment to the descriptions. At the end of the book is a valuable reading list of history for children. An uncommon definition of history is given in the foreword: "History is the mighty Tower of Experience which Time has built amidst the endless fields of bygone ages." Among his earlier writings van Loon showed his devotion to his native country by giving the world a history called *The Fall of the Dutch Republic* and *The Rise of the Dutch Kingdom*. In the book *America,* history is written in pictorial style with many realistic and symbolic illustrations. The story reveals a sense of humor and a practical wisdom suggestive of a Mark Twain, together with a keen knowledge of the facts and a power to present them in a living way.

A dramatic simplicity and directness of expression, a brevity of sentence and paragraph in his *Story of the Bible,* together with a clear understanding and presentation of the subject matter, make the narrative of interest and of value to boys and girls of twelve years and over, and to many an adult. To these it will give a knowledge of and insight into this Greatest of Books, of which so many are in ignorance today. The author said, in reference to the Gospels, "If my little book can give you the desire to read the original, to study these wise parables, to comprehend the immense vision of this greatest of all teachers, I shall not have written in vain. And that is really all I am trying to do."

The Arts, written later, is a most interesting treatise. A review or even an outline cannot be attempted here, but to show its purpose we quote the prefatory statement: "To give the reader a better understanding and a greater appreciation of everything that has been done within the realm of painting and architecture and music and sculpture and the theater and most of the so-called minor arts from the beginning of time until the moment we come so close to them that we begin to lose our perspective." Its dedication reveals the ideal the author held dear—"that all the Arts should have but one single purpose and should contribute as much as it is within their own particular power to do so to the highest of all the Arts—the Art of Living."

Music was one of van Loon's great joys, and he excelled as a violinist. He spoke of joy as the obligation of the race and pointed out how many people strive to be amused but have very little joy. They imagine that fun can be bought, being incapable of making it themselves. Music, he said, is one of the finest media for generating joy in the individual. "Without emotion no art" is one of the oldest of divine laws, and he applied this to the writing of children's books: "like all other good things in life, they should be born out of emotion." Many books have their source in the valley of hope and not on the mountains of enthusiasm; "the result is a product for which my native tongue had an exact expression, 'make Work,' something not born out of the spirit but written under the inspiration of a contract." Then he tells how an early writer poured stories out of the superabundance of his own joy of life. The popularity of van Loon's works is evidenced by the fact that fifty-two translations have been made of them. *The Arts* appeared simultaneously in England, Austria, France and Italy. Others of his books have been published all over the world: in England, Holland, Germany, France, Italy and other European countries; also in China, Japan, India and Brazil. He was the first author ever to receive the John Newbery medal for books written for children.

As to *Van Loon's Geography* we may well say that it is different. There never was one like it. If anyone doubts the author's original way of doing and saying things, let him turn to this book. There is enough fun in it for the writer to say he practices what he preaches —make your own fun. Withal there is more solid fact than most of us know and than most books (on this subject) offer. That it has filled a need is attested by the sale of fifty-eight thousand in a year.

As we look at this man's various products it may be truly said that he has achieved what he set out to do. Reading "between the lines" we suspect a pride in achievement that is perhaps justifiable. There is also a positiveness of statement that at times suggests a dogmatic tendency. However, again and again come sayings worthy of remembrance and quotation, as, for instance, "Wisdom can only be acquired by a constant practice of a reasonable amount of doubt." Van Loon's power to "take off" persons and circumstances would engender bitterness were not the take-off clothed in humor. There was doubtless a vein of irony and satire in his nature. A series of articles in *The Nation* entitled "Speaking of Revolution" shows a humorous satire of affairs and people. In one of these articles the writer seriously notes a condition of the day: "To say that civilization is hell bent for perdition is sheer nonsense. Civilization is merrily galloping toward a great and profound change and that is all. No vital civilization ever came to an end. It continued in some other form. . . . There is no crisis. There is merely a revolution; a revolution which lives faithfully up to its original definition, 'a fundamental reconstruction of the whole fabric of society." *Man the Miracle Maker* shows how through man's many and varied inventions he has become more and more civilized, but he has yet far to go. He has passed from "skin to skyscraper" as a means of protection, from "foot to flying machine" as a means of passage, and there have been many developments in relation to man's hand, mouth, ear and eye, some of which we might not think of. "All inventions," said van Loon, "that have ever been made serve the general purpose of assisting man in his praiseworthy effort to pass through life with a maximum of pleasure in exchange for a minimum of effort."

Discussing in the foreword the hero of this book—Man the Miracle Maker—van Loon pointed out:

> Above all things, he shall say "Yes" to Life and, armed with patience and forbearance and goodnatured humor, he shall relentlessly push forward into the realm of the unknown until the little drop of energy which he has borrowed for a short space of time shall be needed for some other purpose, when he expects to surrender the loan without a single word of regret, as he has learned that both life and death are but expressions of one and the same idea and that nothing really counts in this world except the courage with which the individual dares to attack the one problem to which there is no definite solution, the problem of existence.

In his article entitled "A World Divided Is a World Lost," a sentiment is expressed that may well be remembered:

Of course this is a very small world, so small that it is absolutely impossible for any of us to go through life without doing a little business with the rest of us. Life is a matter of give and take. All we have to do is to learn how to give and take in such a way that both sides shall prosper. For that is the only way in which we can ever hope to establish that definite basis for a mutual and lasting prosperity, without which the world will never come to rest.

Hendrik Willem van Loon followed this philosophy throughout his life, and he has left behind him not only a tremendous amount of writings—books, articles, pamphlets, prefaces, letters—but also the memory of a generous, openhearted man. During the last years of his life he devoted much of his time to aiding war refugees; he was among the originators of the Dutch-language programs over short-wave radio, broadcasting hope and courage to the occupied Netherlands. His great capacity for work never flagged and, when he died suddenly of a heart attack in March of 1944, he had partly finished his forty-second book, the story of his childhood and youth. Its title was *Report to St. Peter.*

Walter Gropius

WHEN the Boston Institute of Contemporary Art displayed models and photographs of the work of Walter Gropius, in a retrospective exhibition in 1952, one popular magazine commented on the surprisingly small number of buildings that this extremely influential architect had erected. With so few buildings to his credit, how could this man have acquired his reputation as one of the foremost of contemporary architects? The answer to this question is provided by an examination of the career of the man who for over thirty-four years had been one of architecture's greatest thinkers and teachers. As founder and director of Germany's *Bauhaus,* which means literally the "house of building," and, later, in America, as head of Harvard's Graduate School of Design, Gropius had developed two of the outstanding architectural schools of modern times. Thousands of students had flocked to these schools to listen to the progressive ideas of Professor Gropius. Later, as architects, they expressed in stone and glass, steel and cement, the modern concepts they had assimilated in the classroom under the master. A new era in architecture had resulted, an era in which the materials and machines of modern industrialism and mass production were fully utilized for the first time in buildings designed to combine usefulness and beauty.

There was yet another reason why the number of buildings that could be called Gropius' was few. The contribution that Gropius has made to modern architecture is as much an attitude as a style. He has been called the "Great Collaborator," and much of his best work exists not in isolated singularity, but as part of the joint effort of fellow architects and students. He firmly believes that the integrated work of a group has a greater potential value than the sum of the work of its members when they work separately. Regarding architecture as "an interpretation of life," he feels that the design of a building should reflect the "intellectual, social, and technical conditions of our time." These conditions create a demand for certain kinds of buildings—factories, for instance, and large-scale housing developments. And the demand is best met, according to Gropius, not by the creative individual anxious to put the stamp of his own personality on his work, but by the co-operative effort of a number of people equally in touch with the conditions. Thus the architect "is to be the brother of the engineer and the manufacturer," whose roles are as important as his own in determining the form that a building will take. The architect's role is distinctive only insofar as he organizes, or puts together in a meaningful whole, the ideas which his brother workers hold in common.

This man, who has so greatly influenced those who are doing our building today, was born in Berlin, Germany, on May 18, 1883. His father, Walter, Sr., was a surveyor in a Berlin suburb. His mother was a lively, intelligent woman who often discussed with young Walter the long tradition of architecture and painting in the Gropius family. At an early age the boy determined upon a career as an architect, and upon his graduation from the gymnasium, or secondary school, in 1903, he promptly enrolled in a technical school in Munich. He progressed rapidly at Munich and was recognized as an exceptional student, but he soon had to leave school for his required military training. Joining a regiment of hussars in 1904, he rose to the rank of corporal in a short time and, before leaving the regiment at the expiration of his period of service, he had been made a Vice-Sergeant Major.

When he was able to return to school, he attended the Berlin Technische Hochschule, an advanced technical school, from 1905 to 1907. It was during this period of training that the young student executed his first independent buildings, being commissioned by his uncle to design some houses for the workmen on his estate in Pomerania. Upon graduating, Walter spent some time visiting Spain, Italy, and England.

Returning to Berlin in 1908, he was appointed head assistant to Professor Peter Behrens, one of his former instructors at the Technische Hochschule.

In 1910 Gropius temporarily abandoned teaching in order to practice architecture. He soon won several commissions, including a factory for the Fagus Shoe Company at Alfeld and settlements for workers at Wittenberg and Frankfort. This early work was distinguished by the use of what were then unusual new building materials. Such things as concrete, aluminum, stainless steel, and great expanses of shining glass were used with great effectiveness. The lines of the buildings were clean and functional, in keeping with the materials employed. Gropius did not clutter his structures with the customary but unnecessary columns, arches, and porches, or with the dull statuary and stone carving so common at the time. Instead, he let his new materials speak for themselves. And they did so eloquently: the bright sparkle of glass; the smooth, urbane gleam of polished steel; and the sinuous curve or stern, sharp angle of poured concrete. So unusual was the work that Gropius was in great demand. He was immediately employed upon several private residences. Later he completed an outstanding group of factories and offices in Cologne.

Soon other architects began to use the materials and methods that Gropius had introduced. A group of them, bound together by certain common characteristics, became known as the creators of a distinctive style: the International Style. Its most important early exponents were Le Corbusier, who was French, Mies Van der Rohe and J. J. P. Oud, who were both Dutch, and Gropius, who, of course, was German. The techniques of the International Style, like its practitioners, were thus not the product of a single country, as the architectural techniques of ancient Greece or Rome or of French Gothic or English Tudor had been. The industrial revolution had been an international development, and its exploitation for serious artistic ends was the aim of this group of architects. These men refused to obscure their new materials with unnecessary decoration, since the textures and forms they worked in were sufficiently decorative in themselves. Nor would they force their designs to conform to a symmetrical scheme, with doors, windows, beams, and pillars formally arranged in a rigid pattern. Instead, they emphasized the rhythms set up by the functional disposition of the building's elements: equally spaced horizontal girders, encircling bands of masonry, the position of such things as elevator shafts and exits and entrances. Moreover, with skeletal steel frameworks, walls no longer had to be massive affairs. They became protective sheaths, often mere curtains of glass delimiting an interior space and permitting a new relationship between the building and its inhabitants and its environment.

It can be seen that it was not alone with the tools and materials created by the industrial revolution that these men were concerned. They were concerned also with the new relationships which that great event had brought about. With man's control over nature increasing, he was able to live at peace with it, no longer hiding behind thick stone walls from sunlight, fresh air, and growing things. And the relationships of men with one another were changing too, though more slowly. Consequently, Gropius and the men of vision responsible for the development of the International Style directed their attention toward the new architectural problems of an industrial age: mass, low-cost housing for workers; safe, efficient factories; spacious stores; comfortable, well-lit offices.

Unfortunately, the activities of Gropius and his fellow artists were soon interrupted by another consequence of the industrial revolution—World War I. Gropius was called up by the German Army. Commissioned as a lieutenant, he was put into a reserve regiment, the Ninth Hussars. At this time Gropius married, but he was able to spend little time with his wife, for his regiment was soon moved to the front lines, where Gropius was wounded in action and was awarded the Mark of Distinction. When he was released from service in 1918, his medals included the Austrian Royal Distinction, the Military Medal of Merit, and the Iron Cross, first and second class.

Before the war Gropius had belonged to the *Deutsche Werkbund,* a craft organization whose purpose had been "to ennoble industrial labor through the co-operation of art, industry, and handicraft." In 1919 he was appointed director of the Staatliches Bauhaus, a state-sponsored school stemming from the older organization. In his book *Staatliches Bauhaus,* Gropius says that the Bauhaus "aimed at the introduction of a new educational method in art and a new artistic concept." Destroying the artist's snobbish prejudice against practical objects made for widespread, everyday use, teachers at the Bauhaus fostered a new respect for the machine and its products. Here, for the first time, students of design were given workshop training. Learning while doing, they became familiar with the materials and machines used in mass production and geared their designs to the utilization of these materials in well-made articles destined for large-scale distribution.

Under Gropius' direction, the Bauhaus was a tremendous success, attracting the foremost artists and the best craftsmen of the time. The school became a center for the creative thought of the '20's. Mies Van der Rohe joined Gropius in training young architects. Internationally famous painters like Paul Klee and Wassily Kandinsky flourished there. Max Breuer, the father of modern furniture design, was on the staff. Boglar and Lindig designed pottery on a mass-production scale. Josef and Anni Albers produced exciting stained glass and magnificent new fabrics. And Bayer and Moholy-Nagy experimented with typography and abstract photography, bringing striking innovations to those fields.

In addition to his executive activities and his teaching, Gropius wrote several books expounding the principles of the Bauhaus. He also continued to build. Several tombs, houses in Berlin and Zehlendorf, a paper factory and a warehouse in Alfeld, and a town theater for Jena were all constructed during this period.

Reactionary opposition to Gropius and the Bauhaus culminated in a charge of "architectural socialism," and threats were leveled against the school and its director by the burghers of Weimar. The more enlightened citizenry of Dessau, anxious to attract the stimulating institution, offered $230,000 and the site for a new school. This offer was accepted, and Gropius designed the new buildings in which the school was to be housed. The famous glass-walled workshop, an outstanding example of the International Style, attracted a great deal of attention when it was dedicated on December 4, 1926. The heart of the school, it was the place where the designs created by the students were "submitted to the ultimate test of determining their adaptability to mechanical mass production."

While serving as director of the Bauhaus, Gropius

was commissioned by the German Government to design a 316-unit experimental housing project in Dessau. The project is notable for its use of concrete on a mass-production scale, and the job stimulated Gropius' interest in low-cost housing developments. Realizing that a healthy environment could help to convert the economically underprivileged into effective and useful members of society, Gropius severed his connection with the Bauhaus and, after a brief visit to the United States in 1928, went to work as director of public housing for the city of Berlin. In that city and in Spandau, Frankfort-on-Main, and Karlsruhe, he built low-cost housing settlements of enormous sociological significance. And from the esthetic point of view these developments were equally significant. As a matter of fact, after examining these projects H. R. Hitchcock reported in his book, *Modern Architecture,* that Gropius did his best work when dealing with problems of social importance.

Of course, anyone who was concerned with human beings and their problems was subject to attack in the Germany of the 1930's. Gropius was no exception. And when in 1934 the Bauhaus was taken over by the Nazis as a school for their vicious leaders, he went into voluntary exile. He went to England first. There he collaborated with Maxwell Fry on a number of residences in London and Kent. He designed the Village

College at Impington and submitted plans to Oxford
University for a new building for Christ Church.
These latter plans were never put into effect, an omis-
sion which the British *Architect's Journal* considered
"a great loss to Britain."

In 1937 Walter Gropius established permanent
residence in the United States. He built a home in
Lincoln, Massachusetts, for himself and his second
wife, whom he had married in 1923 after his first
marriage had ended in divorce. In collaboration with
Marcel Breuer, formerly associated with him at the
Bauhaus, he designed and built a number of residences
in Massachusetts and Pennsylvania. The Hagerty
house in Cohasset, the Abele house in Framingham,
and the Franck house in Pittsburgh are notable examples of his work at this time. He also designed the
Pennsylvania exhibit at the New York World's Fair
of 1939. Black Mountain College in North Carolina
and Wheaton College in Massachusetts were built according to his plans.

In 1937 Gropius joined the faculty of Harvard
University as Senior Professor of Architecture. The
following year he was appointed chairman of the department. Under his inspired teaching Harvard became the leading architectural center in the country,
attracting students from all over the world. But Walter Gropius' service to his new country did not end
with his duties at Harvard. Commissioned by the
government in 1941 to design a defense housing

project, he collaborated with Marcel Breuer on the 250-unit Aluminum City in New Kensington, Pennsylvania. The cost of each unit was a phenomenally low $3280. In 1942 he designed a handsome recreation center at Key West, Florida. In 1946 he was consultant on the plan to rebuild a seven-mile-square area of Chicago's South Side slums. In 1947 he was consultant to General Lucius Clay on a plan for reconstruction work in Germany. He has developed plans for the construction of new townships along superhighways to disperse industry and population from crowded American cities. And he has designed office buildings in Chicago, Boston, and Washington, one such building in the latter city being a radical prismshaped structure with what Gropius calls "eyebrows" —steel and glass louvres that push out horizontally as protection against Washington's scorching summer sun.

Much of the work that Gropius has done in this country has been undertaken in conjunction with the Architects' Collaborative, an organization which he founded in 1946 to further his ideal of co-operative effort in the arts. The Collaborative consists of eight members, whose joint efforts have produced some of the finest buildings of our time. It was the Architects' Collaborative that erected Harvard's magnificent $3,000,000 Graduate Center in 1950. This group of buildings, consisting of seven dormitory units connected by sheltered walks with an imposing community center, is one of the outstanding examples of academic architecture in the country.

In 1953 Walter Gropius resigned from the faculty of Harvard University after sixteen years of teaching there. He continued to work with the Architects' Collaborative, designing six modern schools for Massachusetts and New Hampshire and planning housing developments in Boston and Lexington, Massachusetts. Despite his tremendous influence on American architecture, Gropius is aware that much remains to be done. Commenting upon the present state of American architecture recently, he said: "You go along a big street that is lined for miles and miles with filling stations and restaurants that have absolutely no relationship to the setting, a hodgepodge of ugliness. . . . Or some suburban developer comes along, cutting down trees, bulldozing the site, and befouling our habitat."

However, his realistic appraisal of the situation does not prevent him from being sanguine in his expectations. His own role continues to be an active one, and upon the occasion of his retirement from teaching, he said: "Now for the first time, when I have reached seventy, things look safe for a while. At long last, I am beginning to build much more than was possible in the so-often unsettled past. The coming years should be the happiest and best fulfilled of my entire life."

Philip Murray

THE stock-market crash of October, 1929, signalized for most Americans the beginning of ten years of misery. In the panic that followed that calamitous event 40 billion dollars in securities evaporated and millions of investors lost their life savings. Business houses closed by the thousands. Factories shut down. Banks failed. In the great depression which lasted for ten long years, hundreds of thousands of families lost their homes. At one time there were over 12 million unemployed Americans walking the streets looking in vain for any sort of work. This spectacle was particularly distressing because, as Franklin D. Roosevelt pointed out, plenty was at our doorstep, its use inhibited only by artificial restrictions masquerading as economic "laws." Poverty existed in the midst of abundance because the nation's productive capacity exceeded its capacity to buy. This was largely so because too great a share of the national income was controlled by a small percentage of the population. This income was promptly turned back into investments and savings, while farmers and workers in factory and office were unable to earn a large enough share of our national wealth to buy what they worked so hard to produce.

Fortunately, America was not without great leaders in its hour of crisis. President Roosevelt promised a "new deal" to the nation, and he implemented his promise with specific legislation. But legislation could not do everything. The workers had to organize themselves, to assume sufficient power to match the concentration of wealth which, in the hands of the few, made our economy dangerously unhealthy. Philip Murray, who had come to America from Scotland in his boyhood, provided the leadership which made that work effective. His own conception of the task was an elevated one. "Organization," he said, "fundamentally means . . . clothing and bread and butter and pictures on the walls and carpets on the floors and music in the home and enlarged opportunities for children to receive the benefits of better education. These are the fundamental things, the very roots underlying the foundation of the Congress of Industrial Organization."

Philip Murray, along with John L. Lewis and Sidney Hillman, was one of the founders of the CIO, a vigorous new type of union organization in America designed to restore the country's economic well-being by bringing about, through peaceful means, a greater balance of power between labor and industry. The unions of the CIO accomplished this great end by organizing the workers on an industry-wide basis. These industrial groupings, running horizontally through an entire industry, were a more powerful force than the older type of trade union, whose vertical groupings of the various trades within an industry could be more easily divided. Philip Murray undertook the job of organizing the steelworkers, for steel is America's basic industry and its workers had never been organized even in vertical unions. This was his first assignment with the CIO. Having been a coal man all his life, he knew little of the complex economics of steel when he undertook the job. But his mind, with that affinity for facts which made him so formidable a negotiator, soon mastered the intricacies of steel production and distribution. And his ability to relate these cold industrial statistics to the human needs of the workers—clothing, bread and butter, pictures, carpets, music, education—won him the support of his men. His success in organizing the workers of America's basic industry, according to one social historian, "made industrial unionism an accepted fact," and established the CIO as a social as well as an economic force. His tireless efforts resulted in the formation of the United Steelworkers of America, which was to be the rugged backbone of the CIO, a new force in our country's economic life.

Philip Murray, or Phil as he was known to hun-

dreds of thousands of American workingmen, was no
novice at union affairs when he took on the job of organizing the steel men in 1935. Born in Blantyre,
Scotland, in 1886, he attended his first union meeting
at the age of six, accompanying his father, William
Murray, who worked in the coal mines and was the
president of his local union. Phil's father was a Glad-
stonian liberal who taught him many of his own common sense attitudes toward economic problems. An
Irishman who left his native country for Scotland
when his liberal ideas brought him into conflict with
the repressive British authorities there, William had
married an Irish girl, Rose Ann Layden, whose family
emigrated to Scotland for reasons similar to his own.
Phil's mother died when he was but two years old, his
sister Mary four, and the two children went to live
with their grandfather, Alexander Layden, at Bothwell.

It was at Bothwell that Phil undertook his first
union activity at the ripe age of seven. A great strike
was being carried on in the Bothwell mines in 1893.
It lasted for seventeen weeks, and after school every
day Phil canvassed the town for food for the soup
kitchens set up to feed the hungry strikers' families.
Young Phil had only three more years of school, however, for at the age of ten he entered the mines himself, working full time as a breaker boy for eighty
cents a day. The sum was not large, but it helped.
Phil's father had remarried by this time, and the new

wife brought a young daughter with her into the household. And soon there were other mouths to feed, for new children began to come. Eventually Phil was to have four half brothers and four half sisters in addition to his sister Mary and the little stepsister his father's new wife had brought with her.

With his family growing larger year by year, Phil's father began to think about moving again. He had heard about the wealth of America and, after a preliminary reconnaissance trip, he started out with Phil, in advance of the rest of the family, to set up a home in the new land. Phil and his father arrived in New York, and left Ellis Island on Christmas day, 1902, for the bituminous fields of western Pennsylvania. They got off the train at Irwin and, with their international union transfer cards in their pockets and all of their possessions in a small green trunk which sixteen-year-old Phil toted on his back, they trudged seven miles through the snow to Madison, Pennsylvania, a small Westmoreland County coal town where Phil's Uncle Philip lived. There they settled down and awaited the rest of the family, who joined them the following year.

Phil got a job in the mines, shoveling enough coal to fill three mine cars a day at a dollar a car. At night he studied mathematics and economics. He paid sixty hard-earned dollars for an eighteen-month International Correspondence School Course. So diligently did he work that he completed the year-and-a-half course in six months. During mine lay-offs he played soccer with the men from the pits. He enjoyed the game and played a fair outside left, but his Uncle Phil recalls that he was "too big in the feet" to be a good player. His organizational ability was apparent even then, however, and he managed several teams with some success.

When Phil was eighteen and working for the Keystone Coal and Coke Company in Westmoreland County, he discovered that he and the other men were being short-weighted by a company weight-master. He complained, and the weight-master vigorously denied the charge. As Murray used to tell the story:

> A fight ensued . . . the weight boss took a shot at me with a balance weight. . . . I hit him with a stool over the head. I happened to get the best of the argument, but I was discharged. Some 550 men went out in support of me. Mine guards were thrown around the place; my family was evicted from the company house. That was the beginning of these things that I am interested in.

As a result of young Phil's discovery he was elected president of the local union and led the men in a strike that lasted for four weeks. Finally the strike was broken through hunger. Phil was picked up by a group of deputy sheriffs, who escorted him to Pittsburgh and told him never to return to Westmoreland County.

Phil moved to Hazelkirk, a small, rough mining town south of Pittsburgh. Here he got a job in another coal mine and boarded at the old Red Onion boarding house, where four hundred miners slept in shifts. A prankster in those days, Phil took great delight in tying the toes of sleeping boarders to the bed posts. Another source of rough and ready fun was lining up an audience to watch old John McGary, a fellow miner, struggle into his new-fangled BVD's.

Not long after his arrival in wide-open Hazelkirk, young Phil won election to the job of union check-weighman, a position in which he would be responsible for seeing that the men were not cheated by the company weight-master. Returning to the Red Onion the night after the election, he took a short cut through a mule patch. Halfway across the field he was felled by a blow to the head and pummeled until he was senseless. When he regained consciousness, he dragged himself back to the Red Onion and with three friends set out in search of the 230 pounds of muscle and bone who had opposed him in the election. They found their man and thrashed him soundly. Eight years later, when Phil was elected to the Executive Board of the United Mine Workers, he met the burly miner again. The man admitted that he had been the assailant, congratulated Phil on his election, and both men had a hearty laugh over the episode.

While Phil was working in Hazelkirk he met a girl

named Elizabeth Lavery. She was an orphan, her father having been killed when she was three in an explosion in the Van Voorhis mine. Phil and "Liz" Lavery were married in 1910 in the Roman Catholic Church of the Resurrection in Monongahela City. They returned to the Lavery home for a wedding supper of crackers and cheese with "Aunt Jane," the elder sister who had raised Liz.

Encouraged by his wife, Phil became a naturalized citizen in 1911. His activities in District 5—the Pittsburgh local of the United Mine Workers—had begun upon his first arrival in Hazelkirk. Working with men like Pat Fagan and Van Bittner, the president of the local, Phil's union activities increased through the years. "Sairving" the men, as Murray later admitted in his pleasant Scottish burr, could be dangerous business. He was once hit by a brick while going about union work. And once, while he and Van Bittner were addressing a union meeting, they were rushed by a gang of toughs and pushed into a creek. Such incidents, however, merely provided an added spice to the work of the sturdy, well-built young Murray. He plunged into union work with vigor and quickly rose in District 5, being elected to the International Board of the UMW in 1912, and in 1916 replacing Van Bittner as president of District 5 in an election that proved his popularity with the rank and file.

Murray won national recognition at the early age of 31 when in 1917 he was appointed to President Woodrow Wilson's War Labor Board. In the following year he was also made a member of the National Bituminous Coal Production Commission. President Warren G. Harding continued a policy that was to become standard procedure with Chief Executives when he called on Murray for help in preventing violence in the West Virginia mine fields in 1921. The hot-blooded mountaineers who worked the mines were up in arms. Having been pushed too far, they raised the flag of rebellion, took over telegraph lines, railroad junctions, and signal houses and dared anyone to do anything about it. Violence was imminent. Murray rushed into the thick of things and managed to persuade the miners to put down their squirrel guns. He narrowly escaped serious injury on this mission, for his car slewed off a muddy road and slid down a mountain side.

In 1920 Philip Murray was appointed to the position of vice president of the United Mine Workers by John L. Lewis, who had just assumed the presidency of that organization. This was the beginning of a close twenty-year friendship between the two men, a friendship for which Murray has sometimes been criticized, being called "subservient" or a mere "shadow" of Lewis. No criticism could be more unjust. It is true that Murray worked closely with Lewis

all through the terrible 20's. But the UMW was fighting for its life against political pressure, economic de-
moralization, and the fierce raids of the "Coal and
Iron Police." Unity was essential if the union was to
survive. It did survive those terrible times largely because of the close teamwork of its two top executives.
Lewis of those days has been described as the "far-
seeing strategist and master of psychological warfare." A close observer has said that he would "thun-
der and bluster and threaten the coal operators, then
Philip Murray would move in with his solid array of
facts. A first-rate negotiator, it was Murray who consolidated the gains won by Lewis."

John L. Lewis knew that Philip Murray was worth
far more to the miners than his $9,000-a-year salary.
He once said that Phil knew more about the coal business than $100,000-a-year executives and that none
could compare with him in logical argument. When
the fiery Lewis knocked "Big Bill" Hutcheson of the
Carpenters' Union to the floor of the American Federation of Labor 1935 convention and marched off to
form the Committee for Industrial Organization, he
took Philip Murray with him. The Committee functioned for a time within the parent trade union organization, despite the opposition of some old-time
AFL members. But the differences between the trade
union and the industrial union groups multiplied, and
soon the AFL expelled the Committee. Then it reor-

ganized as the independent Congress of Industrial Organizations, with John L. Lewis as its first president and Philip Murray as vice president, as mentioned above.

In addition to his work in the steel industry, Murray took an active part in unionizing the electrical, rubber, ship, textile and auto industries. In 1940, when John L. Lewis resigned, he was elected president of the CIO. His tenure of office, which lasted until his death at sixty-six on November 9, 1952, was marked by common sense and the spirit of compromise, for the virtues he had learned as a negotiator—moderation, patience, conciliation—stood him in good stead in holding together the forty-odd autonomous unions and five million rank and file members of the CIO.

These same characteristics had won him the respect and admiration of leading industrialists also. At his death he was as warmly praised by the men who had battled against him from the other side of the arbitration table as by the workers in mine and factory who had profited directly from his efforts and who remembered him affectionately as Uncle Phil.

Irving Berlin

IT is 1892. A Jewish family is scurrying through the narrow, twisting streets of the ghetto in Temun, Siberia. In the distance they see a cloud of dust. As the cloud draws near, individual horsemen stand out from it, their drawn sabers glinting cruelly beneath the sun. Cossacks! Shouting with terror, the family flees. Gasping for breath, they reach the fields beyond the town and fling themselves into the ditches, concealing themselves as best they can with branches and dry grass. In a few moments shouts and screams are heard in the distance. Black plumes of smoke leap into the air, laced at their bases with angry tongues of flame. The screams grow louder. More people rush from the town, pursued by horsemen brandishing bloody swords. Few of the running people reach the fields. Those who do are safe, for the horsemen soon tire of their vicious sport, sheath their dripping blades, and ride back to town. Presently it grows quiet upon the plain. And when night falls the family re-enters the town, picking their way among the flaming ruins.

Later in this same year this family of Russian Jews stand huddling together for protection against the biting wind that whistles over the ship on which they are approaching harbor in New York's Upper Bay. Surrounded by boxes and bundles containing all their possessions, Leah and Moses Baline and their eight children look toward the shore, where they will seek a new home in the tenements of lower Manhattan. In the channel a bell tolls mournfully. Gulls screech stridently overhead. Then, with a blast of its whistle, the boat docks, and the Baline family move off, awkward in their shapeless garments, carrying through the winding streets of lower New York the heavy burdens they have brought so far. They have traveled across all of Europe and over the broad Atlantic with the possessions they were able to rescue from their burning town.

Temporary quarters are soon found on Monroe Street, the family later moving to Cherry Street in the heart of New York city's teeming lower East Side. Papa Baline, whose father and grandfather before him had sung the liturgical music of their faith for congregations in their homeland, finds a job as cantor in a New York synagogue. During the week he works in the local butcher shops, certifying meat kosher, or ritually clean, for his Jewish neighbors.

There are many Jews on New York's East Side. There are also many Catholics, Lutherans, and members of the Greek Orthodox Church and of the Russian—for the crowded inhabitants of the area come from many lands, and they have brought with them many faiths. They have also brought a variety of languages, customs, and different manners of dress. Walking through the streets one is struck by this variety, by the color, and by the noise. Above all by the noise! The noise of shouting children at play, of grinding wheels on the cobbled streets, of screams and curses, barking dogs and squalling babies, of peddlers shouting their wares from curbside pushcarts and arguing over prices with buyers, of bells and vans and music. The noise of anger and of joy and of pain. And through it all, night and day, the constant babble of many tongues, speaking many languages in the narrow streets and thin-walled rooms of the crowded tenement district.

It was in this district that Israel, the youngest of the Baline children, grew up. He was four years old when the family arrived in America. And he was soon running in the streets, playing with the other children of the neighborhood. He was known on the East Side as "Izzy." Later he would be known to the world as Irving Berlin.

Young Izzy took to the life of the New York streets readily, playing ball, pitching pennies, swimming in the East River, joining in street gang wars, singing the raucous songs of the day in the delicate

voice which his father had hoped to hear raised in the
spiritual songs of the synagogue. As a matter of fact,
Moses Baline was deeply disappointed in his youngest
son and saddened by his adoption of the tough ways
of the streets. Brought up in the old tradition of European Hebraism, the boy's father was shocked by the
customs of the new land, which allowed so little time
for reading, study, and meditation. He himself had
little enough time for such pursuits now, for he had
taken on a third job to help meet the expenses of bringing up a large family in New York. Anxiety and over-
work soon began to take their toll of his health, and
shortly after his youngest son entered school Moses
Baline fell ill. Then, when the boy was eight years old,
his father died.

Young Izzy was overwhelmed with remorse and
shame at the thought of his own contribution to his
father's burden of worry. During the seven days of
mourning prescribed by Hebrew ritual he determined
that he would make up to his mother for the anguish
he had caused his father. Since the family was now
poorer than ever, Israel, accepting the values of the
new world, decided to devote his time to peddling papers rather than to study. The money he made was
not made easily. Nor was it lightly parted with. Indeed, once he was accidentally knocked into the East
River by the crane of a coal barge, swinging out of
control. Hauled ashore unconscious, the boy still

clutched in his fist the few cents he had earned with his papers. When he returned home that evening, the coins were turned over to his mother without a word, and they helped to swell the little pile that his brothers and sisters earned in the sweatshops of the city.

Leah Baline was less concerned about the material well-being of her family, however, than she was about the intellectual and spiritual development of her youngest son. Remembering her husband, she would often say, "You have the blood of great scholars and rabbis in your veins, Israel. You must never forget that as long as you live."

But young Izzy would forget. He would forget that his mother wanted him to be "a great and famous cantor," and he would sing on street corners for pennies or in local saloons for nickels and dimes, staying later and later as the drinkers asked him to sing more and more songs. Then, as he made his way homeward in the dark, he would often meet his mother, a shawl around her head, searching the streets for him. Once home, she would burst into tears and plead with her son not to do such things. He would renew his promises but soon break them again. Finally, not wishing to hurt his mother but unable to change his ways, Izzy decided to leave home. One evening after supper he walked out of the house, determined not to return until he had "made some *real* money" and could pay for a house, furniture, and servants for his mother. He was fourteen years old at the time.

Izzy spent his first night away from home huddling under the stairway in the dark hall of a nearby tenement house. His second night was spent on a park bench. Then, wandering through the park, he met "Blind Sol," a Bowery character who made a living by singing for whatever audience would drop a few coins in his cup. Since the blind singer needed someone to lead him about, Izzy teamed up with him, getting a quarter for his services at the end of each day. Later, when audiences were sufficiently good-natured and open-handed, the boy was given a chance to demonstrate his own musical talent, pocketing the pennies that his high-pitched young voice drew from the crowd. Soon he was able to give up park benches for the comparative luxury of a hard bed in a cheap hotel room.

Izzy left Blind Sol as soon as he was sufficiently well known on the Bowery to gain an audience by himself. Working alone, he had no one to divide his slender gains with. Moreover, he was free to accept jobs whenever they were offered. Sometimes he would be hired to sing for the evening at Callahan's Bar in Chinatown or at the Chatham Saloon in Doyer Street. He would usually be paid fifty cents for such a night's work. One day the boy was approached by Harry von Tilzer, the composer and music publisher, with a request to "plug" songs for him. This job required that he station himself in the balcony of Tony Pastor's Music Hall in Union Square and rise "spontaneously" to sing additional verses of his employer's songs when they were sung on the stage. For his efforts he was paid five dollars a week by Mr. von Tilzer.

One day while he was walking along the Bowery, Israel met his mother. She prevailed upon him to return home, promising that she would not interfere with what he conceived to be his work. And she did not interfere, not even when he got a job as a singing waiter in Pelham's Café, a Chinatown saloon owned by a big Russian named Mike Salter and frequented by raffish underworld characters. The saloon was also a favorite spot with slumming parties from uptown seeking "atmosphere" in the lower depths of the city. One day while Izzy was working there the place even had a royal visitor: Prince Louis of Battenberg. The visit provided the young singer with the opportunity for a grandiose gesture, for, imitating his boss, who put all the drinks for the royal party "on the house," Izzy refused a five-dollar tip from His Highness with a smile and a sweeping bow. The dramatic interchange between the Prince and the near pauper made headlines in the local newspapers the next day.

But Pelham's Café provided Izzy with the opportunity for more than mere gestures. Spurred on by Mike Salter, he wrote the lyrics for his first song in that saloon. It was provided with a melody by Nick, the pianist at Pelham's, and published by Joseph W. Stern and Company in 1906. Called "Marie From

Sunny Italy," the lyric brought its young composer
the sum of . . . thirty-seven cents. But if the song
did not bring its creator fortune, it did, quite literally,
give him a name. For the title page bore the legend,
"Words by I. Berlin." The name which the young
singing waiter chose as his pen name was soon to echo
round the world.

Irving Berlin (as we shall now have to call him)
ended his career at Pelham's Café quite abruptly. Left
in charge of the place one morning, the tired young
man who had worked through most of the night
drowsed in a chair. Soon he fell asleep. He was awakened abruptly by the proprietor, who had returned
and discovered a deserted bar, his sleeping waiter, and
an empty cash register. The place had been robbed
while Irving napped!

Within a few days, however, Irving had another
job. Working as a singing waiter in Jimmy Kelly's
restaurant on Union Square, he was now close to "Tin
Pan Alley," the home of America's song industry,
which was then located on 28th Street between 5th
and 6th Avenues. And through his lyrics he soon
moved even closer. While working at Jimmy Kelly's
he wrote "Queenie, My Own," "The Best of Friends
Must Part" and "Dorando." The latter song, for
which he received twenty-five dollars, was the first
one for which he wrote the music as well as the words,
making up the tune on the spur of the moment when

a publisher agreed to buy the lyrics if a tune went with them.

But it was as a writer of lyrics that Berlin made his first big commercial success. His next song, "Sadie Salome, Go Home," with music by Edgar Leslie, sold 200,000 copies. And it was as a lyricist that Ted Snyder, the publisher, offered him a contract in 1909, with royalties on all of his published songs and a drawing account of twenty-five dollars a week. The contract ended the young man's career as a singing waiter and made him a regular member of the Tin Pan Alley fraternity. With "a natural flair for words, an instinctive feeling for broad comedy, a rich vein of dialect humor and parody," his humorous songs soon were, in the words of a New York paper of the period, "setting the country wild." Indeed, a single song, "My Wife's Gone to the Country," with music by Ted Snyder and George Whiting sold 300,000 copies.

During the closing years of the nineteenth century and the early years of the present century American popular music was revitalized, largely through the introduction of a variety of African and American Negro rhythms. Ragtime, born in New Orleans of the Negro clog dance known as the rag, was one of the results. Marked by syncopation—transfer of the musical accent to the normally weak part of the measure —and characterized by new tone qualities, novel rhythms and a complete lack of inhibition, ragtime was an unorthodox kind of music. A way of playing as much as a way of writing, its creation was largely the spontaneous product of inspired experimentation on the part of such gifted instrumentalists as "King" Oliver, Nick La Rocca, Buddy Bolden, Sidney Bechet, and others like them. When it was written down, "the rag offered," according to musicologists, "the most intricate and interesting rhythmic development that has ever been recorded in our popular printed sheet music." Such early examples of authentic ragtime as Kerry Mills's "Georgia Camp Meetin'" and Scott Joplin's "Maple Leaf Rag" bear out what the music scholars say about this new type of music. And though the rag was eventually succeeded by other musical styles, its influence continued to be felt in hot jazz, swing, boogiewoogie, and bebop.

Ragtime was also influential in another direction, turning the attention of America from music written to be sung, as most of it formerly had been, to music written to be danced to. The dance craze that swept the country in the wake of the new ragtime soon had the public clamoring for new dance tunes. Tin Pan Alley, never slow to exploit an opportunity, quickly responded. The song that typified that response was "Alexander's Ragtime Band," by Irving Berlin. Like most of the Tin Pan Alley attempts at ragtime, it was a rather feeble and unimaginative imitation of the real thing. This was inevitable, for ragtime was "essentially an instrumental art" produced by musicians who "knew their instruments intimately and exploited their practical potentialities." Berlin, with no knowledge of musical technique, picked out his tunes on the piano with one finger. He was a song writer who wrote a song *about* ragtime. But it caught the popular ear, and Irving Berlin made a fortune on it. He quickly followed up his commercial success with a string of imitation rags, including such numbers as "That Mysterious Rag," "Whistling Rag," "Ragtime Violin," "Everybody's Doin' It," "Everybody Step," and many others. Then, capitalizing upon his newly won reputation, he went on a personal appearance tour, making as much as $1,000 a week in London, where he was billed as "The Ragtime King."

Irving Berlin's name was now one to conjure with, and he was soon being sought after by such people as Florenz Ziegfeld, the producer of Broadway's most elaborate extravaganzas. Irving was to write music for more than one production of the *Ziegfeld Follies*. In addition, he had become a partner in the music publishing firm of Ted Snyder, the publisher of his early songs. With the royalties on his songs added to his other sources of income, he was now a wealthy man, earning well over $100,000 a year. The boy who had once run away from home to "make *real* money" had achieved his goal. He was able to provide his mother with a house, fine furniture, servants, and many other luxuries. And with his mother provided for, he decided to get married.

The story of Irving Berlin's first marriage is a brief and pathetic one. In February, 1912, Irving married Dorothy Goetz, the beautiful young sister of a song-writing friend. The couple went to Cuba on their honeymoon and returned to an expensively furnished home on Riverside Drive, overlooking the Hudson River in New York. Early in July Dorothy came down with what appeared to be a cold. By the fourteenth of the month she was dead of typhoid fever, which had been contracted in Cuba. Berlin was, of course, grief-stricken. But even his grief was turned to financial gain. Out of his sorrow, he composed "When I Lost You" a sentimental ballad which enjoyed a tremendous success. It was the prototype of many of the composer's most famous songs.

When America entered World War I in 1918, Irving Berlin tried to get a special assignment to entertain troops. Before his request was acted upon, he was drafted. But when he reported for basic training at Camp Upton, near Yaphank, Long Island, he was assigned to a special job. Promoted to sergeant, he was put in charge of a fund-raising soldier's show. The show, *Yip, Yip, Yaphank*, with script and lyrics by Berlin and with an all-G.I. cast, opened in New York on July 26, 1918. With war enthusiasm at its peak, the show was a tremendous success, making over

$80,000 and establishing one Berlin song, "Oh, How I Hate to Get Up in the Morning!" as the national lament of our citizen army.

When the war ended, Irving Berlin went on an ambitious personal appearance tour of the leading vaudeville theaters, singing his own songs at a salary of $2,000 a week. He also established his own music publishing firm, Irving Berlin, Inc. And he continued writing songs, producing one of his most popular numbers, "A Pretty Girl Is Like a Melody," for the *Ziegfeld Follies* of 1919. Becoming more and more interested in the theater, he added yet another lucrative activity to his already crowded career. In partnership with Sam Harris, the producer, he built the Music Box Theatre, which opened in 1921. Berlin's first show, *The Music Box Revue,* with songs like "Say It with Music" and "Everybody Step," grossed over $2,000,000. New editions of the show followed year after year with like success, Berlin writing such hit tunes for them as "Always," "What'll I Do," "All Alone," and "Remember."

Irving Berlin was now making over $500,000 a week, an income that brought with it a vast amount of social prestige. Meeting people highly placed in the social scale, he became acquainted with Ellin Mackay, whose father was Clarence H. Mackay, the head of Postal Telegraph, and who was heiress to a fortune of $30,000,000. The friendship gradually ripened and

before long the boy from the slums of the East Side
and the girl who had been brought up on a sumptu-
ous Long Island estate were deeply in love. One major
obstacle stood in the way of their marriage: Ellin's
father. The socially conscious old man would not accept a slum-born son-in-law even if he was a famous
song writer and a millionaire in his own right. He
was adamant. Finally, when Ellin realized that her
pleas would never win her father over, she decided to
elope with Irving. The couple were married in City
Hall, New York, on January 4, 1926.

When the news of the elopement reached Ellin's
father, he disinherited his daughter and refused ever
to see her again. Neither the birth of her first child,
in November, nor the death, two years later, of her
new-born son softened the old man's heart. It was not
until 1929, when the stock-market crash swept away
most of the Mackay fortune, that a reconciliation between father and daughter finally took place. Eventually the stubborn old man even came to respect and
finally to admire his son-in-law.

The stock-market crash that had undermined the
Mackay fortune also wiped out Irving Berlin's newly
acquired investments. Besides, the popular demand
for Berlin tunes fell off sharply at just about the same
time. Irving became despondent, losing for once his
aggressive enthusiasm. With it went his marvelous facility for turning out hits. In 1927 he had written

three smash hits, "Blue Skies," "Russian Lullaby," and "The Song Is Ended." The year 1928 saw both a falling off in output and a diminution of the song-writer's popularity. A year passed without a single tune being ground out of "Buick," Berlin's trick piano with the attachment that enabled him to transpose melodies mechanically from F, the only key in which he could play. Another year passed, and Buick still remained idle. Then another. Along Broadway the wiseacres were saying that Berlin was through.

Then, in 1932, Rudy Vallee, the radio crooner, revived "Say It Isn't So," an old Berlin tune. It caught on, and Berlin, encouraged, dug an old unpublished manuscript out of his files. "How Deep Is the Ocean?" it was called, and it too was a success. Nevertheless, when his friend Sam Harris asked him to write the score for a new musical he was producing, Irving was skeptical about his ability to continue to satisfy popular taste. He decided to accept the job, however, considering it a test. The show was called *As Thousands Cheer*. A landmark in Berlin's career, it was a tremendous success, containing such songs as "Heat Wave," "Maybe I Love You Too Much," "Not for All the Rice in China," and the perennially popular "Easter Parade."

Since *As Thousands Cheer* Irving Berlin has enjoyed continued success as a songwriter. He has written close to a thousand songs during his long career, most of them hit tunes selling thousands of copies for months, some even for years. Actually, all that music is not fresh and original. Berlin admits that he has used six or eight of his best tunes over and over again. "White Christmas," for instance, is "Easter Parade" written in thirds. Try it on your piano and see. As a matter of fact, "Easter Parade" itself is a rewriting of a song called "Smile and Show Your Dimple," which Berlin wrote in 1917.

Naturally, *As Thousands Cheer* was not Irving Berlin's final score for the stage. Since then he has written much lively theater music, including that for *Louisiana Purchase, Annie Get Your Gun,* and *Miss Liberty.* Attracted to Hollywood soon after talking pictures were born, he wrote the music for *The Coconuts* and *Puttin' on the Ritz.* Then, with Fred Astaire dancing to his tunes, he won new popularity with musicals like *Top Hat* (1935), *Follow the Fleet* (1936), and *On the Avenue* (1937). A picture based on his first big song hit, "Alexander's Ragtime Band," was a success in 1938. More recently he has written the music for such films as *Second Fiddle, Holiday Inn, Blue Skies,* and *Easter Parade.*

Cannily, Irving Berlin refuses to sell his music to the theater and the movies. He rents it, instead. Thus, controlling the rights to his songs, he is able to double his income from them, for he collects royalties as well as rental fees on them. And the royalties are aug-

mented through the rental, since the songs are popularized by their use on stage and screen. Though he is
now enormously wealthy, the point of view that he
adopted in the slums of New York, when he determined to "make *real* money," still dominates his
thinking. In Hollywood his crafty bargaining won
him a contract calling for 10 per cent of the gross income from each picture on which he works. *Alexander's Ragtime Band* brought him $36,000 under
this arrangement, and on *Holiday Inn* he made almost
as much. Despite this large percentage, however, he
refused to allow all of the songs from the latter picture to be released for publication at once. To have
done so would have forced them into competition
with one another, thus reducing their potential value
as money-makers.

Yet despite Irving Berlin's reputation as a tight-
fisted businessman more interested in making *real*
money than good music, he has contributed an enormous amount of his time, energy, and money to his
adopted land. During the Second World War, for instance, he duplicated his World War I success with a
spectacular GI show called *This Is the Army*. For it he
wrote such favorite wartime tunes as "I Left My
Heart at the Stage-Door Canteen," "The Army's
Made a Man Out of Me," and "I'm Getting Tired So
I Can Sleep." In addition, he spent time directing the
show and appearing in it, singing his old hit, "Oh,

How I Hate to Get Up in the Morning!" After a successful New York run, the show toured the world for three years, making over $10,000,000, every penny of which went to the Army Relief Fund.

Berlin has also written songs for other American institutions and for various branches of the armed services, the proceeds from each of these songs has been donated to the organizations involved. "I Threw a Kiss in the Ocean," for instance, brought close to $15,000 to the Navy Relief Fund. "Arms for the Love of America" was devoted to the Army Ordnance Association. "Any Bonds Today?" helped the wartime bond drive to succeed. The American Red Cross was aided by Berlin's "Angels of Mercy," and "The President's Birthday Ball" helped spark the March of Dimes campaign against infantile paralysis. Perhaps the most sensational of his efforts in this direction was his allocation to the Boy Scouts, the Girl Scouts, and the Campfire Girls of all the royalties on the patriotic song "God Bless America." The sum involved was over $100,000.

Actually, there is a broad streak of sentiment in the hard-boiled little music maker from the lower East Side, a streak of sentiment that he has frequently cashed in on in his music. Life in the slums taught him to cash in on everything, and he learned his lesson well. But in learning it, he did not forget the country that had provided him and his family with a refuge from oppression. He has given America a great deal of pleasant music. He has also given her, from time to time, something that she long ago taught him to value even more highly—impressive sums of cold, hard cash.

Both gifts have been widely appreciated. On February 18, 1955, a medal especially authorized by Congress was bestowed on Irving Berlin by the President. It was presented to the composer "in national recognition and appreciation of services" to his adopted country.

Knute Kenneth Rockne

IN 1893 from an obscure hamlet in Norway a five-year-old youngster with his mother and sisters started on a great trip to America. He was a descendant of the Vikings, with, it may be, a strain of Irish blood in his veins. In 1931 that Viking youngster had grown to be the greatest football coach in the United States and a man admired and beloved by thousands. At his death columns of the great cities' newspapers were devoted to him and his achievements.

Why such honors for Knute Kenneth Rockne when there were many football coaches in the country over whom there would not have been so much ado?

He himself attributed to his ancestry a possible first reason for what he attained. He was descended from Enidride Erlandson of Losna, Norway. When Queen Margaret of Norway merged the three Scandinavian kingdoms into one, the Erlandsons, who were large landowners, retired to establish themselves among the hills. The venturesomeness of Rockne's father broke out when the boy was five, and the Chicago World's Fair was in progress. The father was an engineer with carriage building as an avocation; ambitious to exhibit his work at the Fair, he traveled to Chicago, then sent for wife and children. Rockne has spoken with pride of his mother who brought the family without a mishap into the heart of the country, knowing not a word of English. He calls this first step in Americanization "one of a million minor miracles" indicative "of the stuff and fabric of America." He refers to "his only equipment, a Norwegian vocabulary, a memory of home cooking and of skiing and skating in the Voss Mountains." His first encounter with natives was with the aborigines, a group of Indians. Rockne wrote in *Collier's Magazine* of how a tow-headed Norwegian youngster got lost in the Elysium of the World's Fair. His father, elated by an award for his carriage, had failed to check the boy's curiosity, so that he wandered until he landed at a facsimile of an Indian reservation. "The white-haired Nordic, fresh from the original source of supply," made a striking contrast to the jet-haired Indian papooses with whom he stayed till morning. Then a cop discovered "a blond head surmounted by feathers, bobbing through a scampering mob of Indian kids, wielding a wooden tomahawk and yelling for scalps." He was soon stripped of his Indian finery and restored to his parents.

Rockne's childhood and youth were spent pleasantly in Chicago. Stories are told of contests with boys, Irish and Swedes in the Logan Square district—often with "baptisms of mud." His parents looked on football as "a system of modified massacre" and forbade it. But Rockne joined the Barefoot Athletic Club of older boys, mostly Irish, and one day scars of battle gave evidence of a surreptitious game. His football career was squelched for the time being. Spring came and with it a gang for baseball. To use Rockne's words, "Blessed or bothered by hidden strains of Irish ancestry, I found myself in the thick of it." A bat bent the bridge of his nose. He went home blinded, but uppermost in his mind was the reflection, "The family banned football because it is dangerous. And I got this nose from baseball."

Undoubtedly an athletically minded youth, when high school days came he went out for football with parental approval. At thirteen, weighing one hundred and ten pounds, he was put into the scrubs. During the summer, seeking to earn some money while developing their bodies for football, Rockne and a teammate got jobs cleaning the school windows at good pay. Other boys broke the windows, entered the building, bent on destruction. The culprits escaped, but the window cleaners, suspected of the intrusion, were accused and fired.

During the school term, when not playing second-string football, Rockne trained himself at track and pole-vaulting, winning some reputation and making the Chicago Athletic Association Junior team. Soon track and field events began to supplant his interest in football, and he was admitted to the Illinois Athletic Club.

There came four years between high school and college when he was obliged to earn a living. He had a couple of years of night work. Then, planning to go to the University of Illinois, he set himself to save one thousand dollars. Though at the time a clerk could earn only one hundred dollars a month and it took a year to learn the dispatching system, Rockne took a civil service examination for mail service and became a mail dispatcher. He was called a fool for "tackling a tough job," but he persisted, encouraged by a sister who was, he acknowledged, more ambitious for him than he was for himself.

Two of his friends were studying at Notre Dame in South Bend, Indiana, and they suggested that he accompany them instead of going to Illinois. Notre Dame then meant nothing to Rockne, but on investigation he found that he could "get a job and get by cheaper," and so he went. Sensitive and sometimes easily depressed, he acknowledged "the strangeness of being a lone Norse Protestant invading a Catholic stronghold." That was in 1910, when he first arrived at the college. Even then, however, the city boy was strongly impressed by the site of Notre Dame, with its two thousand acres and its many beautiful trees. In

1925, no longer "a lone Norse Protestant," his reception into the Catholic Church occurred in the beautiful Sacred Heart Church of Notre Dame.

During his college career his father died and he thought then that college and football must end for him. Again his sister interposed and urged him to persevere. He remained at college and, excelling in chemistry, as a senior he was appointed an instructor in that subject. This might have been his lifework, but football held the greater interest.

In 1913, his senior year, Rockne was made captain of the team under Jesse Harper, a man whom he never forgot and to whom he owed much. Rockne and Charlie Dorais, the quarterback who was his roommate, worked hard all that summer, perfecting their game and practicing a new play for the fall football season. They held their surprise for the game with Army, a team never before beaten by Notre Dame and a heavy favorite to win. Then they launched a forward-pass attack that bewildered the Army's defense and brought victory and fame to the formerly insignificant midwestern college. The forward pass had been somewhat haphazardly and unskillfully used previous to this time. But Rockne brought it suddenly and dramatically into the forefront of football news, having painstakingly perfected its technique in long summer practice sessions with Dorais. The football world was amazed, and the game was revolutionized.

This contest was the evidence of the great strategist Rockne was to become. After his graduation in 1914, he remained at Notre Dame as assistant coach, and in 1918 became head coach. As a teacher and trainer he excelled. The universal testimony is that "Rockne's record is one of the most remarkable that any coach of any sport has ever piled up." He introduced into the game new features, brought the back field shift to a high development, and gave a new conception of line play. He advocated the open game which is generally accepted today.

Of even greater importance than his contributions to the game were the ideals of clean sportsmanship which he encouraged and the influence which he exercised over his men. An indefatigable worker, intense and courageous, he believed in hard work and had no sympathy with "softness." Some people, however, think he put too great a value on sports. Perhaps he did, for the growth of large-scale athleticism in our centers of higher education reflects his influence. One educator, noting this trend, observed, "In many American colleges it is possible for a boy to win twelve letters without learning how to write one."

In fairness to Rockne, it must be said that he attempted to elicit the best qualities of sportsmanship. In discussing intercollegiate sport, he once said, "If they are not careful, they will have this nation 'softening up.' The kids are all right yet, in spite of the

automobile and sorority teas and week-end parties in
the city. But this growing attitude is beginning to be
felt in many of the colleges and universities at that.
The most effective antidote is intercollegiate football,
and it's about time that some of these people begin to
realize it." But even those who accept Rockne's somewhat primitive, Spartan attitude have questioned the
methods which he encouraged because, through emphasis on the training of a handful of men for large-
scale, professionalized competition, the athletic activity of a major portion of the student body was,
inevitably, overlooked. The spectator in the grand-
stand, however great his team spirit may be, does not
get a great deal of exercise.

Whatever we may think of Rockne's attitude
toward sports, we must admit that he understood his
boys and tried to bring out the best in them. They
worshiped their "Rock" as a god. But he was not a
driver as the term is generally understood. He was
economical of emotional effort, and had a psychological understanding of persons and situations. His
teams on the field were cool and competent. Robert
Harron of the *New York Evening Post* pointed out
four milestones in his leadership in football. The first
was the Notre Dame–Army game of 1913; the second, the two great seasons of 1919 and 1920 with un-
defeated campaigns, when Knute Rockne became a
national figure. The third was when his "Four Horse-

men" team illustrated his genius in 1924. Each of the four, Stuhldreyer, Miller, Leyden, and Crowley, in his own way contributed to success. From East, South, and West they took the laurels.

Traveling great distances as Rockne's teams did, they obtained the name of Rockne's Ramblers. During 1925–28 successes were not so constant, though there were not many defeats until the last of these years. Rockne hated defeat, for he was not an easy loser, but through it all was a good sportsman. Of all things he disliked tie games. In his thirteen-year coaching record there were 122 games, 105 of them victories, 12 defeats, and 5 draws. He had power to transfer an idea from his mind into the minds of others—a secret of success. He felt that his boys could win, he made *them* feel that they could win, and they did win.

In 1929–30 came the fourth and final milestone and this was a brilliant ending with the team now called the "Rockne Raiders." In both seasons they had not a single defeat, although these were both "tough campaigns."

In 1929, on probably the coldest football day New York had ever seen, 80,000 watched Army and Notre Dame fight another tense battle on a field frozen so hard that cleats wouldn't hold. It was the last game of a season that had found Indiana, Navy, Wisconsin, Georgia Tech, Carnegie Tech, Drake,

Southern California, and Northwestern falling in order before this machine that had Carideo at the throttle.

Possibly the Rockne Raiders "fought" the better because of their devotion to their great leader, who was ill that year with "thrombosis-phlebitis" and for all but three of the games was bed-ridden; against the wishes of his physicians he attended these three in a wheel chair. At other times by telephone calls to the team and to Tom Lieb, his quarterback who was in charge, Rockne directed the campaign almost as thoroughly as when he was well. In a wheel chair he continued to carry on his duties as coach.

Of course at Notre Dame he had done a good deal of work outside of regular coaching, and the strain had been great. There were summer-school coaching sessions that took him all over the country. Furthermore he was a prolific writer and his articles for newspapers and magazines were constantly in demand, besides frequent public speaking which he enjoyed. In 1928 he took a group of students to the Olympic Games. He also planned the new stadium at Notre Dame which is a lasting monument to him. For some outside undertakings of a commercial nature he was criticized. Rockne's comment was:

> In my writing and all the other work I have done, in addition to the coaching, I have been honest. I have written my own stuff to the papers. I have taught the

best football I know in any coaching schools. I have been honest with Notre Dame and I have considered that my first duty is to provide as well as possible for my family against the day when I won't be coaching football teams and when they won't be buying my stuff in the newspapers and magazines. And when the day comes that they think another coach can do a better job, I intend to be able to say a pleasant good-bye and carry away with me as few worries as possible.

Knute Rockne was devoted to his family, and his devotion was recognized and appreciated by the people of South Bend among whom he lived. He and his wife, Bonnie Skiles Rockne, whom he married in 1914, and their four children, William, Knute Jr., Mary Jean, and Jack, are still remembered with affection in the town as a happy family group. Rockne's love for his mother continued to be a strong tie throughout his life. In an article which he wrote for publication he recalled how in the early days he had taken his mother to Notre Dame to see him play. She had by then seen him in action on the football field many times, but, he reflected, "A boy wants his mother to see him at his best." He performed wonderfully for her that day. For his sister Rockne also nourished a tender feeling. It was she who had encouraged him in days of ill fortune, and when he achieved fame he was not slow to acknowledge publicly the part she had played in shaping his career.

At one time Rockne had been told by his physicians

that he had only about three years to live. But his health had improved and he was working hard when he was killed in an airplane crash on March 31, 1931. Forty-three years of dramatic life, ending with dramatic death! And this at the peak of his success! Perhaps this hard, ambitious man would have chosen such a death for himself.

From the airplane wreck in Kansas all that was mortal of Knute Kenneth Rockne, the "Rock of Notre Dame," was taken back, to be laid in Highland Cemetery, not far from the campus. Thousands came from far and near to the memorial service. King Haakon of Norway sent a consular official to represent him at the funeral; President Hoover expressed his condolences; and Ex-President Coolidge also paid his tribute.

Speaking of Rockne's amazing football career, Burt Chamberlain, who had known him well, said, ". . . he was one of the few men who could win and keep on winning and still retain a deserved reputation for clean playing." And Tom Lieb, one of Notre Dame's great quarterbacks, expressed the feeling of all of Rockne's boys when he said, "He was more than a teacher of football; he was a father to all of us at Notre Dame."

Igor Sikorsky

O VER a thousand years ago somewhere in China an unknown artisan, obsessed with the fanciful notion of making a heavy object rise into the thin air, invented the Chinese top. The toy, a marvelous gadget, was lifted high above the earth when its whirling propeller was set in motion by a shaft that the operator spun between the palms of his hands. This toy was the world's first flying machine.

Hundreds of years later Leonardo da Vinci, the famous Italian painter and inventor, rediscovered the principle underlying the Chinese top and designed a spiral air screw capable of rising into the air. The principle, of course, was that of the helicopter, a machine that takes its name from two Greek words: *helix,* meaning "spiral," and *pteron,* meaning "wing."

Other attempts to conquer space through the use of a device that would bite into the air and pull a heavy body upward followed. Small models using bird feathers and springs were developed and flown. In the 1870's a successful seven-pound steam-driven machine incorporating the principle of Da Vinci's air

screw took to the air. Several attempts were even
made at building a machine large enough to bear a
man aloft. But all of these attempts failed.

Few people knew about these curious experiments.
Few knew that Da Vinci had ever done anything but
paint his wonderful pictures. Or, if they knew, they
didn't care, for the man's paintings were so important
that, by comparison, anything else he might have accomplished paled to insignificance. But late in the
nineteenth century the wife of a university professor
in the Russian city of Kiev became interested in
Da Vinci. She studied the painter's notebooks, fascinated by his wonderfully fertile mind. And by the
time her youngest son, who was born in 1889, reached
the tell-me-a-story age, she was so full of the exciting
notebooks that she began to amuse her boy by talking
about Da Vinci instead of telling him about the imaginary creatures in the Russian fairy tales. The boy,
whose name was Igor Ivan Sikorsky, remembered the
strange things his mother told him, particularly those
concerning Da Vinci's spiral screw. He remembered
so well, in fact, that by the time he was twelve years
old he had constructed a small helicopter himself.
Powered by rubber bands, the little machine actually
flew!

As young Igor grew up he continued his experiments in mechanics. He was primarily interested in
flying machines, but he tinkered with all sorts of

gadgets in the little home workshop behind the house in Kiev. As a matter of fact, when he was but thirteen years old, he constructed a small bomb which he detonated in the back yard. A crew of workmen on a nearby building project stopped to watch the boy. Later they described what they had seen to the contractor on the job, who, in turn, told Igor's father. Professor Sikorsky listened attentively to what he was told, thanked his informant, and returned home. But instead of scolding his son, he praised him for his experiments and told him to continue with them. Igor, encouraged by his understanding father, spent more and more time in the little workshop, eventually producing there such complex contrivances as a steam-driven motorcycle.

At school Igor was a good student, and he was accepted for enrollment in the St. Petersburg Naval College in 1903. Graduating from the college in 1906, he refused the offer of a commission in the Navy and returned to Kiev. There he entered the Polytechnic Institute, bent on becoming an engineer. But he soon discovered that the theory of mechanics was not nearly so exciting as was tinkering with machines. And as there was no tinkering and much theorizing at the Institute, Igor became bored and left without taking his degree. Perhaps news about the famous American experiments of the Wright brothers, who had made their first successful airplane flight in 1903, or about the early dirigible flights of Count Zeppelin, had hastened his decision to quit the stuffy Institute. At any rate, he was soon on his way to Paris, then the European center for aeronautical experimentation, to learn all he could about the practical business of building aircraft.

In Paris young Sikorsky discovered that building aircraft was far from being a practical venture. In 1909 the man who went high enough to "break wood," that is, to have a crash, was a creature to be regarded with awe and respect. When Igor asked a French aviator to name the best aircraft engine, he was told, "They are all bad!"

Intent upon acquiring the components of a plane, Igor persisted. "Which is least bad?" he asked.

"The one with the smallest number of parts," was the answer, "for the parts are all bad, too."

Another piece of advice that Igor picked up in Paris was more helpful, and he has always remembered it. Drawn into conversation with a Captain Ferber there, he described his own early experiments in airplane design, perhaps bragging a bit. The Captain eyed him briefly, smiled, and replied concisely, "To invent a flying machine is nothing; to build it is little; to make it fly is everything."

Igor returned to Kiev somewhat chastened. But his spirit was not completely depressed, for he had purchased, despite the warning of his pessimistic aviator friend, a three-cylinder, twenty-five-horse-power Anzani engine. And when he got back to his workshop, he started to build a helicopter to use it in, financed in the work by his sister Olga. Of course, when the craft was completed it did not fly. But Igor was still not depressed. Far from it. He was exuberant, for when he attached his machine to a scale and raced the engine he discovered that it lifted 375 pounds—only 100 pounds less than the weight of the machine!

A second attempt at building a helicopter proved no more successful than the first, and Igor turned his attention to the sort of aircraft that was then establishing itself as the conventional type. But his airplane was as much of a failure as his helicopter. And when a second airplane that he built failed to leave the ground, people began to call him a crackpot and to snicker at his crazy ideas. Nevertheless, some of his friends had faith in him, and with the aid of two or three student engineers whom he had studied with at the Institute and a plumber and two carpenters who were interested in his experiments, he rebuilt his plane, which he called the S-2. Finally, he met with success. On June 3, 1910, after days of taxiing in the neighboring fields, the S-2 took to the air. It soared four feet above the ground for twelve seconds, traveling almost 200 yards while aloft! Before the end of the month Sikorsky had piled up almost eight minutes of flying time in his wonderful machine. Then, on June

30, he climbed eighty feet above the earth in the plane
and attempted a turn. The machine stalled, hung
sickeningly in the air for a moment and plummeted
to the ground like a stricken bird. The S-2 was completely demolished, and Sikorsky was almost killed.
But he survived the crash, and when he recovered he
went back to work on another plane.

Igor's father, who had always been interested in his
son's work was impressed by the boy's accomplishment and by his persistence in the face of discouragement. Now he decided to help the boy by providing
him with as much capital as he could spare. Thus,
aided by his father as well as by his sister, Igor continued his aeronautical experiments, eventually producing the S-5. On its first flight this machine climbed
to an altitude of 300 feet and, after staying in the air
for four minutes, made a perfect landing. By 1911,
Igor had reached 1,000 feet in the S-5, remaining
aloft for a half hour. He had also obtained a pilot's
license from the Imperial Aeronautical Club of Russia and had been presented to the Czar after participating in the maneuvers of the Russian Army with his
plane. And in the same year, 1911, the young aviator
set a world record, flying the S-5 at the then terrifying
speed of 75 m.p.h. while carrying three passengers.

It was while flying the S-5 that Igor Sikorsky got
the idea that was to establish him as one of the foremost designers of multi-engine aircraft. And the idea

was spawned by a mosquito! One of those pestiferous insects got into the gasoline line of the S-5 and was drawn into the carburetor, stalling the machine and necessitating a forced landing. Sikorsky reasoned that a plane with more than one engine would have been capable of continued flight if such an accident had incapacitated one source of power. In addition, of course, the plane would have added power in normal flight, making it capable of carrying greater loads at higher speeds. Designing such a plane, he won the highest award at the Moscow Aircraft Exhibition of 1912. He also won a contract with the Russo-Baltic Railroad Car Works, as chief designer for their aircraft division. The contract contained a provision which specified that Sikorsky could build one experimental plane a year at company expense. At last he had adequate financial backing for large-scale experimentation. And his salary enabled him to pay back the money his family had contributed to his work. By this time the sum amounted to over $25,000.

Sikorsky's first experimental plane for the Russo-Baltic Car Works was called the *Grand*. Weighing 9,000 pounds and having a 92-foot wing span, it was the first four-motor dual-control airplane ever built. In it Sikorsky established another world record in 1913 by staying aloft for one hour and fifty-four minutes with eight passengers aboard. The plane was later inspected by Czar Nicholas II, who was so delighted with it that he presented its designer with a gold watch bearing on its case an outline in diamonds of the two-headed imperial eagle. Sikorsky, who still believes in the possibility of restoring the Russian monarchy, wears the watch on special ceremonial occasions to this very day. The *Grand,* however, was long ago destroyed. The accident in which it was demolished was a freak one, occurring as the airplane sat idle on an airport runway. Another plane was flying in the area at the time, and as it roared over the *Grand,* its engine dropped out, falling on Sikorsky's plane and smashing it to bits.

The Russian airplane builder was soon at work on another plane. When he had completed it in 1914, accompanied by two co-pilots and a mechanic he took it on a 1500 mile flight from St. Petersburg to Kiev and back. One bit of excitement broke the monotony of the epic flight. Indeed, it almost ended the trip, the plane, and its occupants' lives. A fire suddenly broke out in the big plane as it sped over the bleak Russian steppes. It flared brightly, dangerously close to the fuel supply. Quickly, Sikorsky stripped off the heavy overcoat he was wearing as protection against the biting cold. He fell on the fire with it and, the other members of his crew following suit, the flames were soon extinguished, allowing them to complete the trip without further incident.

During World War I Sikorsky built military aircraft for the Russian government. A bomber version of his multi-engine plane was the first aircraft to carry and drop thousand-pound bombs on enemy troops and installations. Later in the war Sikorsky added defensive armament to his 17,000-pound bomber. With eleven strategically placed machine guns jutting from apertures in the plane, it seemed to contemporaries that it bristled with guns. In all, Sikorsky supplied 74 bombers to the Russian Army, selling them to the government at $125,000 each. By the end of the war he was a wealthy man, leaving over $500,000 in bonds and real estate when he fled the country at the outbreak of the Russian Revolution.

Like many Russian *émigrés* at the time of the Revolution, Sikorsky took refuge in Paris. After a brief stay he moved on to London. Then, in March of 1919, he came to America. Possessing only $600 when he arrived in this country, the famous plane designer immediately sought work in the aircraft industry. But in post-war America there was no aircraft industry, or next to none, for a business slump had reduced airplane production to a bare minimum. Without work, Sikorsky was soon reduced to a diet of bread and beans. A part-time job in a settlement house on New York's East Side, where he taught Russian immigrants aviation, mathematics and astronomy, earned him from three to ten dollars a week. It also helped him to learn English. And in the settlement house he met Elizabeth Semion, who was to become his second wife. His first wife, whom he had married in Russia when he was still little more than a boy, had died before he left his homeland, leaving him with a young daughter to care for. As the years passed, Elizabeth, whom he married in New York on January 27, 1924, presented him with four fine sons.

Backed by a small loan from a man named W. A. Barry, Sikorsky had in 1923 begun working on his first American plane. Construction was started in an abandoned chicken coop on a farm near Roosevelt Field, Long Island, a group of Russian friends working without pay to help the designer. Sometimes it was so cold in the makeshift workshop that the men's fingers froze to the metal they were working with. But even though they used second-hand materials and made their own tools, the devoted group soon exhausted their funds. Then Sergei Rachmaninoff, the musician, was induced to invest $5,000 in return for a vice-presidency in the newly organized Sikorsky Aeronautical Engineering Corporation. The money enabled the men to rent a hangar and complete their work on the two-engine plane. In May, 1924, the S-29, as it was called, took off on its test flight. Eight men who had worked on the plane crowded aboard, anxious to participate in its first flight. The overloaded plane lurched across the field and staggered into the air, but the strain was too much for its second-hand motors. They sputtered, coughed, died; and the plane came crashing down in an empty field.

The S-29 was badly damaged, but it was not completely demolished. Sikorsky knew that it could be rebuilt and made to fly if he had a little more money. But there was no more money—unless! He called a hurried meeting of the stockholders of the small corporation. When the stockholders had all assembled, Sikorsky locked the door of the meeting room, pocketed the key, and sat down. He was determined to rebuild his plane, and unless the stockholders provided the capital needed for the completion of the job, he wasn't going to open that door. Such a procedure was outrageous! Sikorsky was using coercion! He was guilty, actually, of kidnaping! He wasn't going to be allowed to get away with such high-handed methods! But before the door of the meeting room was opened $2,500 had been raised.

The sum proved to be sufficient. Sikorsky went to work on the plane, enlarging it so that it was capable of carrying fourteen passengers at speeds of up to 115 miles per hour. When it was completely rebuilt, Sikorsky chartered it as a passenger and transport plane, making over 200 flights in it before he sold it to Roscoe Turner, the stunt flyer, in 1926. Turner used the plane as a flying emporium for United Cigar Stores for years, finally selling it to Howard Hughes for use as a German bomber in the moving picture "Hell's

Angels." When the old crate was intentionally set afire and wrecked in the movie, it had logged over 500,000 miles!

Having built one of the first successful twin-engine planes in America, Sikorsky won more substantial financial backing. In 1925, with new capital, he reorganized his company as the Sikorsky Manufacturing Company. Still experimenting, he next built the first tri-motor plane produced in America. Then he turned to a radically new type of aircraft—the amphibian. His S-38, a two-engine, ten-seat amphibian, was a peculiar-looking aircraft. Its hull, wings, and tail were separate and distinct elements, joined only by struts. Old-time pilots seeing it fly over would shout, "There go the spare parts of a Sikorsky, flying in formation!" But the S-38 was a sturdy workhorse of a plane, and it opened new horizons for the aviation industry. Martin Johnson used two Sikorsky amphibians to film *Wings Over Africa*. Lindbergh inaugurated air-mail service between the United States and Panama with one. And, using thirty S-38's, Pan American Airways pioneered its air-travel system in South America. In addition, the planes, which cost from $20,000 to $150,000, were sold to many wealthy American sportsmen as private flying expanded during the postwar boom in America. In all, Sikorsky sold over 100 S-38's, realizing a fortune on them.

The stock-market crash of 1929 that brought ruin to so many American businessmen did not hurt Sikorsky. One month before the crash occurred, he had sold his newly organized Sikorsky Aviation Corporation to United Aircraft. Through the sale it became known as United Aircraft's Vought-Sikorsky Aircraft Division. The noted designer did not become an executive in the new corporation. Caring little for the financial manipulations characteristic of big business, he chose instead to continue contributing to the practical end of the industry, taking a job as engineering manager of the new division. With the proceeds from the sale of his company and a $25,000-a-year job in the new organization, he was naturally wealthy enough to indulge some of his idiosyncrasies. On his ten-acre estate in Newton, Connecticut, he built a small observatory and renewed his interest in astronomy. He took up farming as well, raising cucumbers, which he is fond of. He is also fond of tractors—he owns three—and of volcanoes, sometimes traveling thousands of miles to see one of the latter in action.

A more serious side of Sikorsky's life away from the aircraft factory is revealed by his purchase of a comfortable old farmhouse located near Easton, Connecticut. This is his private hideaway, where he goes when he wants to be undisturbed so that he can indulge his contemplative bent. To this side of his life belong the religious and philosophical books that he has written, including *The Message of the Lord's Prayer,* which has been called "a beautifully written expression of deep religious feelings"; *The Invisible Encounter;* and his autobiography, *The Story of the Winged S.*

Actually, however, Sikorsky still spends most of his time on aeronautical research. He puts in six hours a day at the factory in Stratford, near Bridgeport, Connecticut. In addition, he spends from two to five more hours a day on problems which he brings home with him. It was Sikorsky who designed the $30,000 wind-tunnel for the Vought-Sikorsky plant. And it was Sikorsky, of course, who brought world fame to the company and himself by designing the enormous clippers, or flying boats, that pioneered in establishing regular service over both oceans. The twenty-ton S-42, which Sikorsky built in 1934, was the largest flying boat of its day. Capable of carrying 32 passengers and a crew of five, it broke ten world's records for speed, altitude, and pay load, and proved to airplane manufacturers like Martin and Boeing that aircraft could be both large and economical. One particular economy that Sikorsky's research was responsible for was the reduction of the wing span of large aircraft with a consequent increase of wing load, or amount of weight borne by each square foot of wing. Ridiculing the idea that a light wing load was essential to safety, the Russian-born designer observed: "The albatross rides the storm with perfect ease, but just see what happens to the butterfly with its light wing load. It is blown away."

Having built some of the world's largest aircraft with relatively short wings, Sikorsky now decided to build small craft with no wings at all! He still remembered his mother's talks about Da Vinci's spiral air screw. And he determined to build a helicopter, despite his early failures with the type. Interest in craft of this sort had been revived by the invention of the autogiro, the first practical departure from the fixed wing airplane. But the autogiro, a compromise between an airplane and a true helicopter, was little more than an aerial curiosity. It could not ascend vertically, for its free-spinning windmill-like rotor was unpowered. The engine merely drove a conventional propeller which provided forward motion, causing the rotor to revolve and lift the plane into the air. Sikorsky decided to build a true helicopter. And after years of research and an outlay of $300,000, on September 14, 1939, his experiments reached fruition. On that day the V-S 300, a wingless framework of welded iron pipe equipped with a 75-horsepower engine, was lifted vertically into the air by its single whirling rotor. A new era in aviation history had begun.

There was, however, some delay in getting started. On its first flight the VS-300 had risen only a few

inches from the ground. It was not until the spring of
1940 that Sikorsky took the machine up for its first
sustained flight. It did *almost* everything he wanted it
to do. It ascended and descended vertically. It hovered
motionless in mid-air. It flew to the right and the left.
It even flew backward. There was only one thing it
would not do. It would not fly forward! Spectators
laughed derisively, calling the helicopter "Igor's
folly." Soon, though, they were of a different mind.
Before Pearl Harbor Sikorsky had ironed out all of the
"bugs" in his 'copter. During the war it was used ex-
tensively for liaison, reconnaissance and aerial rescue
work. By the time of the Korean conflict the helicopter had developed tremendously, and the "egg-
beater," as the UN troops called it, proved an invaluable asset in the mountainous and swampy terrain of
Korea. Over one thousand crashed pilots were rescued
from behind enemy lines by the little "whirlybirds."
Twenty thousand casualties were evacuated by 'copter. In addition, the helicopter laid mines; hauled
troops, weapons, and supplies; strung wire; recon-
noitered, and did a thousand and one military jobs.

And it is not military service alone that the helicopter offers. Capable of utilizing roof-top landing
spaces, the helicopter can provide fast shuttle service
between outlying airports and cities. It has been used
for mail and passenger service, for rescue and police
work, for short-haul freight and for aerial photog-

raphy. As a crop duster the helicopter is safer and more efficient than conventional planes. And an aerial cowboy has even used a helicopter on his 500,000-acre Texas cattle ranch, halving his branding time and paying for his machine out of savings in six months' time.

In our fast-changing world, it seems as though the helicopter is destined to make some of the greatest changes yet. The convertiplane, that will whirl aloft on a rotor and transform itself into a speedy jet in mid-air, is just over the horizon. Soon, perhaps, we shall be seeking a 'copter in every roof-top heliport, and rotor blades will be as common a sight as television antennas against the sky. The idea may sound fanciful, but ask Mother and Dad if they ever thought, when they were your age, that they would one day see twenty-ton flying boats linking continents. Ask Granddad, if, as a boy, he could have conceived of man soaring through space. Igor Sikorsky is probably just about Granddad's age now, and when he was a boy he had visions of such things. One of the few pioneers of aviation who is still alive, he still has visions. Perhaps before he dies he will translate a few more of those visions into reality.

George Grosz

IN 1938 a ruddy-complexioned artist with dark hair, regular features, and piercing blue eyes became an American citizen. Upon receiving his naturalization papers, he exclaimed, in imperfect English, "It is the fulfillment of a wish dream. I had it since I was nine." The artist's name was George Grosz, and his dream had been fostered by a youthful reading of James Fenimore Cooper's *The Last of the Mohicans*. The dream had been intensified by Grosz's exposure to the ugly conditions of life in Germany during and after World War I. So preoccupied with the thought of America did Grosz become that, as a young artist living in Berlin, he drew pictures of the New York skyline before he had ever seen it. In other pictures, with Cooper's book in mind, he drew himself in the likeness of an American Indian. And, intent upon learning all that he could about American ways, he often followed tourists from Chicago and New York about Berlin, observing their behavior until they grew suspicious of him.

In 1932, when Grosz finally arrived in America, he

was an outcast whose works were banned in Hitler's Germany. Already a world-famed artist, his line drawings had been compared with the best work of Dürer, Bosch, Goya, Hogarth, and Daumier. He was the master of a trenchant style which was said to be "as perfect an instrument of social satire as had been developed in centuries." However, as a resident of the land he had so long dreamed of, he found less need for satire than he had felt in pre-Nazi Germany. He temporarily abandoned the weapon he had mastered and concentrated on idyllic landscapes in water color and figure studies in oil. He developed a water-color technique of his own, applying pigment on wet paper so that colors would blur and "bloom," producing effects that were, in part, accidental. But the work of the artist who had drawn "the most definitive catalogue of man's depravity in history" did not long remain serene. Grosz began to mirror some of the turmoil of his disturbed personality in his landscapes. Eventually the skill that had produced, in the German drawings "a nearly perfect record of a period" was turned inward to lay bare the "satanic currents" that "force the world to disaster." The results are what Grosz called "Hell Pictures," and critics, recognizing him as "one of the world's great artists," liken his later works to macabre medieval paintings of the lower regions.

Grosz, who was born in Berlin on July 26, 1893,

first began to sketch at the age of five, imitating his father, who idled away the time in his unsuccessful restaurant by making sketches on the tablecloths and on cardboard beer coasters. Young George's early subjects were usually battle scenes, which he copied out of illustrated news magazines depicting German colonial warfare in South Africa. When his father's restaurant eventually failed, in 1898, Grosz's family moved to Stölp, in Pomerania, where George's father acted as caretaker of a Masonic Lodge building. The young artist's initiation into the macabre and the grotesque began there. He long remembered the story some of his playmates told him at that time of a skeleton guarded by two mechanical monsters, concealed in a secret inner chamber of the Masonic Lodge building. These young storytellers elaborated on their invention with fiendish delight, telling their frightened playmate that anyone who discovered the secret room would be crushed in the steel embrace of the monsters. However, young George's fear soon wore off, and he was fascinated by the giant canvas panoramas which he saw at country fairs in Pomerania: one showed a mother with an insane gleam in her eyes devouring a dismembered child; another showed an erupting volcano showering human limbs in the air. These gory spectacles failed to disturb the boy, but they did stick in his mind, and when one of his older sisters gave him a set of oils, one Christmas, he painted from memory a picture of "Napoleon in Hell" which he had seen at a fair.

When Grosz was seven years old his father died, leaving George, his mother, and two sisters nearly destitute. The family returned to Berlin, where Mrs. Grosz tried to provide for her children and herself by working as a seamstress. But her meager earnings could not support three children, and within a year the family was back in Stölp, an ugly garrison town filled with coarse, brutal soldiers. Mrs. Grosz, as a stewardess in an Army officer's club, worked hard to keep her children in bread and shoes and send them to school.

Despite his mother's hard work, the school young George attended was inadequate, and he was far from happy there. He was taught little, and his instructors were bullies. One teacher, Herr Knap, a former Prussian Army officer, was particularly vicious. His method of punishing any infraction of school discipline was to force the offending student to stand before him at rigid attention while he turned the top of a heavy signet ring into the palm of his hand with deliberate slowness. Then, suddenly, he would strike the boy square in the face with all of his force. George Grosz learned early that "the law of life was blow and bite." But he was a boy who was not easily cowed. One day when it came his turn to stand before Herr Knap he flung up his arm as the ring hand descended, grabbed the teacher's wrist, and threw him over his shoulder into the middle of the room. Herr Knap landed in a heap with a severely strained back. Grosz, who had been taking a correspondence course in jujitsu, was expelled from the school.

One day after his expulsion from school George told his mother that he wanted to be an artist. The hard-working woman reproached him bitterly, saying, "Remember that nothing counts but money." But despite her bitterness, his mother's opposition to his plans soon relented, and at the age of sixteen George left Stölp for Dresden and the State Art Academy. He spent two years at the Academy, wearily copying plaster casts while the carefully husbanded supply of money with which his mother provided him shrank steadily. Young Grosz could earn next to nothing himself, for no one ever bought his drawings. He began to despair. But when *Ulk,* the comic supplement of a weekly Berlin paper, bought one of his caricatures for thirteen marks, his hope rose again. After selling a few more drawings, he left the Dresden Academy and went to Paris to study under better teachers. Later he went to Berlin, where he worked with Professor Emil Orlik in the School of Applied Arts.

Grosz was just getting started as an artist when his career was interrupted by World War I. He was drafted for service in 1914 and sent into action almost immediately. Marching through Belgium with the garlanded troops of the invading German Army, he had a premonition of disaster when he saw the flowers that the soldiers were decked with wither. A year in the trenches, overwhelmed by the horror of war, convinced him that his premonition had been correct. Then, suffering from shell shock and battle fatigue, he was hospitalized. While in the hospital he resumed his graphic work, expressing the horror and stupidity of war in drawings that were published in several magazines. But the German high command, discovering his satirical sketches, recalled him to active service in 1917. Seeing no sense in the butchery of "a world gone blind and delirious," Grosz rebelled against his orders. He was arrested and, despite his previous honorable service, was tried as a treacherous malingerer. Subjected to extreme humiliation at the hands of callous officers, he was eventually thrown out of the army, branded as mentally unstable.

Choking with rage and resentment at his treatment and at the thought of "a civilization that could produce and condone such bestiality," Grosz released his pent-up hatred in a flood of drawings. At first the targets of his pencil were the ruling hierarchy of the state and the Prussian Junkers, who were the officer class of the German Army. Soon, however, he realized that society was honeycombed with corruption. He was particularly nauseated by the activities of the middle class, which had profiteered throughout the war and was still scrambling for advantage at any cost in the face of all the misery that defeat had brought. In his drawings Grosz attacked the dense, greedy middle class; the fatuous priests who were its apologists; the vicious politicians and armed thugs who were its protectors. He recorded the corruption he saw in such drawings as "The Mighty Toad," which shows fat profiteers gorging themselves with food in the presence of starving bystanders, and "Five in the Morning," a two-panel drawing showing miners plodding to work on one side while, on the other side, their exploiters spew the ingredients of a night's revelry from surfeited stomachs.

Reprisals followed such attacks on the pillars of society. Grosz was arrested three times in a period of eight years. He was fined over 6500 marks for publishing drawings that were condemned as inimical to morals and critical of the army. Nor were the reprisals limited to official measures, for Grosz was often threatened with personal violence. On one occasion an army man, seeing Grosz in a restaurant, shot at him, narrowly missing him and wounding a waiter. Twice Grosz was attacked by knife-wielding fanatics who resented his drawings. So fierce was the antagonism that, at one point in his career, Grosz couldn't walk down the street unless he was surrounded by a cordon of his friends.

These were terrible times in Germany. The Weimar Republic was disintegrating, and the forces of reaction were taking over. Cabinet members like Erzberger and Rathenau were murdered in cold blood by the fast-growing Nazis. Violence was universal. Recalling the period, Grosz says, "A broken chair leg with blood on it became the symbol of my neighborhood." But Grosz could not be intimidated. He had aptly characterized himself in a bit of verse during his student days:

> Look! Here comes Grosz!
> The saddest man in all the world.
> But he is no craven dog.
> He is a tough guy
> And wears his hat at an aggressive slant.

He had to be a tough guy to survive during those times.

But Grosz did more than merely survive. In bitter line drawings, which he published, he attacked Hindenburg, Ludendorff and the increasingly powerful Hitler. He caricatured industrialists like Krupp and Thyssen, who robbed the poor and supported Hitler's vicious thugs. He pictured the starving soldiers who begged for bread while the rich glutted themselves. He saw workers being slaughtered for daring to strike, and he put such scenes on canvas or paper. At great peril, he followed the Storm Troopers on their nightly rounds of violence. And he illustrated their activities in his drawings. "That'll Learn 'Em," for instance, shows a horribly bloody professor being dragged from his home by three Storm Troopers. "A Writer, Is He?" depicts a man being held against a wall with a machine gun in his belly while his room is searched. And "No Echo Here" is a picture of a man out in the country, where he has been brought by Hitler's men for execution.

But the Nazis and the forces that supported them were not to be stopped by drawings, however savage those drawings might be. And in 1932, just before Hitler gained absolute power in Germany, Grosz fled to the United States. He had escaped just in time, for he was the primary cultural target of the new Führer, being designated "Cultural Bolshevist No. 1" and having his works banned in Germany by proclamation. All of his thirteen volumes of published drawings were confiscated, and the plates from which they had been printed were destroyed. But Grosz had produced over 3,000 drawings before he left Germany, and these were now widely distributed. Many copies of his books had also passed beyond the borders of Germany. Of these books, the volume called *Ecce Homo*, published in 1923, is perhaps best known. It consists of a series of thirty drawings of "the robbers, the exploiters of human souls, the double-dealers, and the dealers in death," and its savage indignation brought Grosz world fame.

Despite his reputation, however, all was not to be

smooth sailing for Grosz—not even in America. He had left Germany in a hurry, taking very little with him. Having a wife and two young sons to support, he was badly in need of a job. John Sloan, a fellow artist, urged him to come to the Art Students League in New York to teach. But the board of the school, at the instigation of the arch-conservative Jonas Lie, objected to Grosz. Blind to the evil at work in the world and frightened of the courage that dared face it, they called Grosz an "unhealthy influence" and refused to hire him. Sloan resigned from the school in disgust. But the students, neither blind nor dumb, raised a clamor, and eventually Grosz was engaged.

Grosz remained at the Art Students League for the rest of his teaching career, teaching twice a week. He also gave six lectures a year for the Department of Architecture at Columbia University. But by far the busiest part of his life was spent at home, in the studio —once a bedroom—of his two-story stucco house in Douglaston, L.I., or later in The Cottage at Hilaire Farm, in Huntington, L.I. There he painted from nine to six, often forgetting the thermos bottle of coffee or the sandwiches his wife would bring him for lunch every day. He was a swift worker, spending about an hour on a drawing, two hours on a water color, and from one to three months on an oil. Working at this rate, he estimated that he had filled hundreds of sketchbooks during his years as an active painter. In addition, he completed many thousands of finished drawings and water colors, and hundreds of oil paintings. His works are hung in such places as the Metropolitan and Whitney Art Museums in New York, the Detroit Institute of Art, the Los Angeles Museum, the Art Institute of Chicago, the Duncan Phillips Memorial Gallery in Washington, D.C., and in many other distinguished collections throughout the country.

Grosz was happy in America, his boyhood dreams of the United States being amplified rather than marred by contact with reality. Indeed, he said that his "romantic sense was in no way disappointed" by what he found here. His later works often take familiar American scenes and people for their subjects. Skyscrapers, the O. Henry characters whom Grosz saw in New York, and the landscape of Cape Cod where the artist spent his summers, appear in many of his drawings and paintings. But Grosz realized that evil is not limited by national boundaries. Though he strove to achieve a balance in his work, he couldn't help but feel that the "satanic currents that force the world to disaster" are predominant everywhere today. Such works as "Piece of My World" (of which there are two versions, one more horrible than the other), "No Let Up," and "I Woke Up One Night and Saw a Burning House" have been called "tapestries of utter ruin." And a late water color of a ragged veteran lying watchfully in a ditch, armed to the teeth, provides, perhaps, Grosz's ultimate comment on the prospects of civilization as we know it. For Grosz's lone, battered soldier in a desolated and unpeopled landscape represents the world worn down by wars to its last man. But he no longer menaces George Grosz, who died on July 6, 1959.

Raymond Loewy

"I HAVE always believed," says the French-born designer Raymond Loewy, "that society could be industrialized without becoming ugly, and this has been my ruling philosophy." In pursuing his ideal, Loewy has become "the Mr. Big of industrial design." Indeed, he has been credited with the invention of that profession. But, having transformed the appearance of many objects produced by American industry, Loewy is content to let others have the credit for inventing the profession, which, according to him, combines "the functions of the artist, engineer, and silent salesman," making manufactured articles handsome as well as useful. Loewy makes a great deal of money through his own skillful combination of the functions of artist, engineer, and salesman, grossing close to $3,000,000 annually. But despite his tremendous profits, he claims, "It is a poor designer who cannot save his clients more than the fee they pay him." In illustration, he can point to the markedly increased volume of sales of almost every product upon which he has been consulted.

Loewy has been charged with being more concerned with creating striking designs to encourage an increase in sales than with creating designs of enduring beauty. Critics point out his addiction to streamlined forms, noting that such shapes are appropriate in objects like airplanes, where wind resistance is a significant factor, but inappropriate in the wide variety of products in which Loewy has used them. He defends his idiosyncrasy, asserting that the streamlined form satisfies "a craving for tidiness and simplification" even when it has no practical function. He is aware that sensational designs can be used to disguise the faults of technically shoddy products, but he condemns such practices as unethical. "No reputable member of the profession," he says, "would offer a design that was less sound than he could make it within the limits of cost, available materials, and public taste."

Loewy himself has done a great deal toward overcoming these limits. He has convinced executives that they "must give major consideration to esthetics." The result has been a great increase in industrial budget allotments for design improvement. Indicative of this trend was the Pennsylvania Railroad's allocation of $18,000,000 for a series of experimental locomotives designed by Loewy in 1934. As for materials, Loewy has overcome many of the prejudices formerly governing their choice. His extensive use of plastics, for instance, has helped to popularize them and has resulted in the expansion of the plastics industry. And in defiance of maritime traditions, he has designed all-metal ship interiors, thus reducing fire hazards and insuring liners like the *Panama* and the *Christobel,* whose staterooms he designed, against the flaming fate of the *Morro Castle.* Even public taste has been radically altered by Loewy, for the simplicity of his designs has encouraged a popular revolt against the inelegant designs with which industry so long flooded the country.

Loewy's concern with good design is no mere part-time or business interest. It is a lifelong preoccupation. As a matter of fact, so deep-seated is his attitude that as a young soldier in World War I he designed and cut his own uniform rather than go into battle in the awkward and ill-fitting general-issue uniform. And his dugout was the best decorated one on the Western Front, being carpeted, draped, and wall-papered with soothing Parisian materials. Despite his concern with clothes and furnishings, however, Loewy's war record in the French Army was outstanding. Trained as an engineer, he was awarded the Croix de Guerre for snaking across no-man's land to plant wires for ground communication within twelve feet of the German trenches. Severely burned in a mustard-gas attack at Reims, Loewy was saved by a young American ambulance driver. Upon his recovery he was made a captain. And by the end of the war he had acquired seven decorations for valor.

Even before the war, Loewy's interest in good design was apparent. In 1906, at the age of thirteen, he won the J. Gordon Bennett Medal for a model airplane that he designed and built. During the medal competition his plane established a distance record by its one-minute flight in the Bois de Boulogne, near his home in Paris. Previous to winning the Bennett medal, Loewy's interests had been literary. At the age of twelve he had edited and published a magazine, encouraged by his father Maximilian, a Viennese gentleman noted as a writer on finance. However, the boy later decided to become an engineer. When he finished his secondary schooling at Chaptal Collège, in 1910, he enrolled for a course in engineering at L'Ecole de Lanneau. Undoubtedly his mother approved of this practical course. She was a hard-headed French provincial who berated her husband for his improvidence and countered his visionary advice to young Raymond and his two older brothers with the oft-repeated suggestion that it was "Far better to be envied than pitied." Apparently the boys heeded her advice, for all three are now substantial citizens of the United States: Maximilian, Jr., as a banker; Georges as a surgeon; and Raymond as head of Raymond Loewy Associates, a five-man partnership with over 300 clients, a staff of 200, and a gross annual business running into millions of dollars.

Raymond Loewy came to the United States shortly after World War I, during which both of his parents had died. One of his brothers, already in America, had promised to get him a job as an engineer with the General Electric Company if he should come to New York. Raymond, whose training had been interrupted by the war, went back to L'Ecole de Lanneau, graduating in 1919. Then he left for America, taking with him his engineering degree, his captain's commission in the French Army, a handful of medals, and—nothing else. After he had paid for his passage he was so broke that when he was asked to contribute to a war relief charity social on the boat, he had nothing to give. He did a quick sketch of a beautifully dressed woman and contributed that. This sketch marked a turning point in his career, for it later sold at auction for $150. Loewy, amazed, decided to abandon engineering for the more lucrative field of fashion illustration.

The magazine *Vogue* provided Loewy with his first opportunity as a fashion illustrator. Later he worked for *Harper's Bazaar* and for New York department stores such as Saks Fifth Avenue, doing window displays as well as fashion advertisements. His illustrations were marked by an innovation that has since become an advertising cliché: the use of a simple figure strategically placed in a sea of white space. The device was extremely effective in advertising layouts; however, when Loewy tried to apply the technique to window display, he was not uniformly successful. Saks encouraged his experiments, but when he displayed a single mannikin in Macy's window, he was immediately fired. Macy, unlike Saks, depended upon a large volume of business and could not afford to sacrifice space for the added emphasis which Loewy's arrangement gained.

In 1926, Loewy was asked to redesign a printing machine for a manufacturer. He took the machine to his apartment and worked on it in his spare time. Modifying the machine considerably, he eliminated unnecessary parts and simplified others, thus making it easier to operate and to repair. This was his first attempt at industrial design, and both he and the manufacturer were pleased with the results. Abandoning advertising, Loewy went in for industrial design on a large scale, redesigning automobiles, office equipment, household appliances, and many other products. As he tells it, one job just led to another until, today, he spends much of his time warding off new business.

Loewy's first big commercial success in industrial design was the Coldspot Refrigerator, which he executed for Sears Roebuck and Company in 1934. A completely new departure in refrigerator design, the Coldspot eliminated the unsightly, dust-catching motor housing, the motor being concealed in the base of the refrigerator. The design boosted Sears' refrigerator sales by over 135,000 units in three years and won first prize at the Paris International Exposition in 1937.

Loewy also won a gold medal at the Paris Exposition for his contributions toward improved transportation. The locomotives which he had designed for the Pennsylvania Railroad in 1934 represented a radical new approach to train design. Cumbersome smokestacks and antiquated cowcatchers were discarded. Projecting headlamps and whistles were embedded in an enveloping metal sheath whose sleek contours covered the entire engine. This sheath lacked the 2000-odd rivets that studded old-time engines, for its seams were welded, presenting no obstacle to the rush of the wind over its streamlined surface. Attached to an old-fashioned string of block-like cars, Loewy's new engine would have been as ineffectual as a polished arrowhead on an untrimmed stick. So Loewy designed streamlined cars of gleaming metal that whistled along behind his locomotives like polished shafts from a well-strung bow.

Not content with improving the exterior of the train, Loewy went to work on the inside. Before he had finished he had transformed the traditionally dingy coaches, pullmans, club cars and compartments. Even the dining car was affected. Indeed, one of the railroad traveler's main sources of irritation was eliminated, for Loewy designed non-spill coffee cups for his high-speed train. On a Loewy-designed train the traveler could save time . . . and his vest.

Railroads were not the only medium of transportation to receive Loewy's attention. The Greyhound Bus Lines called upon him for his help. After riding hundreds of miles on buses to determine what improvements could be made in their design, Loewy developed a spacious new three-level model with body-conforming seats, washroom, water-cooler, and clear-view compartment for the driver. Long-distance travel in such buses is not the torture that cramping seats and infrequent stops once made it.

Truck drivers also have benefited by Loewy's activities. When the International Harvester Company employed him to modify the design of their trucks, he incorporated many features that add to the comfort and safety of the driver. Such things as arm-rests and storage compartments for personal belongings and cross-ventilating provisions for the cab of the truck are Loewy innovations. So too is the support built into the seat to protect the battered kidneys of long-distance truckers.

More recently, Loewy has invaded other sections of the transportation industry. The gray-and-green interiors of Constellation airplanes are the result of Loewy's recommendations, for his investigations led him to believe that such a color scheme would act as a deterrent to air-sickness. And following World

War II, the first basic automobile design improvements were made by the Studebaker Corporation, following Loewy's suggestions. These improvements included: greater all-around visibility through an increased window area; the use of black light in the dash panel for safer night driving; and a more comfortable rear seat suspended between the axles rather than, in the traditional position, over the rear axle.

The transportation industry is not, of course, Loewy's sole interest. He has designed everything from lipstick cases to supermarkets. His clients have ranged from those who wanted a new label to put on a bottle (Roma Wine), to those who wanted him to redesign a chain of stores (W. T. Grant and Company). He has designed terminals as well as buses for the Greyhound Bus Lines. Streetcar firms and tooth paste manufacturers have engaged his services. He has designed housings for electric shavers (Schick), packages for cigarettes (Lucky Strike), and caps for pens (Eversharp.) A few years ago he was employed to do all the designing—from soap wrappers to retail stores—for Great Britain's 500-unit, globe-girdling Unilever Company. His fee for this latter job has not been revealed, but in the past he has demanded retainers ranging from $2000 to $200,000, in addition to costs for his staff's time and for materials. It has been estimated that the yearly sale of Loewy-designed products runs to something over $3 billion.

Raymond Loewy Associates, in turn, nets well over $3,000,000 a year, half of this sum going to Raymond Loewy himself. With so large an income, Loewy can afford to spend a couple of months in each of the six luxurious homes he owns, scattered from Southern California to Southern France. He can afford the three dozen suits that make him one of America's best-dressed men. And he can afford such expensive affectations as a solid-gold cigarette holder and such costly hobbies as deep-sea diving. This hobby, incidentally, is a far more costly one for Loewy than for most of its devotees. Formerly diving was spoiled for the sensitive-nosed Loewy by the smell of oil from the pumping apparatus. But now he explores the deep with unoffended olfactories, for he mixes the oil in the pump with Chanel No. 5!

Loewy, with his expensive and eccentric tastes, is, of course, aware that other factors besides pure need create a demand for consumer goods. He lists three such factors:

1. the American urge to replace,
2. the psychological compulsion to keep up with the Joneses,
3. salesmanship.

He admits that as an industrial designer he exploits these three factors. *Never Leave Well Enough Alone,* the title of his autobiography, is a confession of the extent of his exploitation. He does agree that some products have progressed beyond the improvement stage. It would hardly be possible, for instance, to improve the design of the common needle. And he does observe some taboos. For example, when he was asked to help a builder of grave vaults, he declined, saying, "I cannot improve upon death." But the limits which he imposes upon himself are as few as his profits are great.

Perhaps the curious character and career of Raymond Loewy can best be disclosed by a final illustration. It concerns a $50,000 bet that Loewy proposed to the late George Washington Hill, tight-fisted head of the American Tobacco Company. Loewy's bet was that he could improve the green Lucky Strike package and that, as a result, Hill would sell more cigarettes, without changing their quality. His improvements consisted of a change in the package color, from green to white, on the theory that since people put cigarettes in their mouths they like to see them in a sanitary-looking container. He also discarded the printed matter that had occupied one side of the pack, reproducing the bull's-eye trademark on both sides. Thus when a smoker threw an empty pack away, the brand would be advertised, no matter which side of the pack was exposed. These two minor changes in package design and no change in the quality of the product brought a marked increase in sales. So Loewy won his $50,000!

Spyros Skouras

THE story of Spyros (pronounced Spear-o) Skouras' life is almost as fantastic as the plot of one of the forty-odd pictures which his Twentieth Century Fox Film Corporation produces every year. It began in the year 1893 in Greece, in the small town of Skourohien, or Skourasville as it would be called in America. The town had been founded by Spyros' grandfather in 1830, during the Greek War of Independence against the Turks. But the family did not prosper, for the small village on the Ionian Sea was beset by "Mediterranean Worm," which ruined the vineyards. One year during heavy rains the village dam broke, flooding the Skouras farm and leaving it covered with sand and stones when the waters receded. Panagiotes Skouras, Spyros' father, was unlucky in another particular also: half of his ten children were girls for whom dowries had to be provided, and one of his sons died in infancy.

Under these circumstances the four remaining sons had to be put to work at an early age. Spyros, who had been destined for the priesthood, at thirteen left school for a job in nearby Patras. He worked as a printer's helper and later as an office boy in an insurance and navigation company. His older brother Charles emigrated to America, hoping to mend the family fortunes in the land where the streets were paved with gold. He started work as a bus boy at the Jefferson Hotel in St. Louis. When he had risen to the position of bartender, at a salary of $8 a week plus $25 in tips, he sent passage money to Spyros and upon his arrival in St. Louis in 1910, got him a job as bus boy at the Planters Hotel. The following year the two boys sent for their young brother George. Demetrios, the eldest brother, remained in Skourohien to rehabilitate the farm.

In America, Spyros' sixteen-hour day began at 3:45 a.m., when he presented himself to Frank Balzar, the bartender of the Planters Hotel. Balzar was a patriotic and energetic individual who insisted upon Spyros' joining him in singing the *Star-Spangled Banner* at the start of each day to improve his English and display his patriotism for his new country. After this early-morning rendition of the national anthem, Spyros began his work. He broke up twelve large blocks of ice, half into lumps for highballs, half into shaved ice for cocktails. Next he swept up and prepared the place for customers who would begin arriving at ten o'clock. He then doubled as a waiter until four o'clock. In the evening he studied English,

shorthand, accounting, and commercial law at Jones
Commercial College. By the time he got to bed his
feet were often so sore that patches of skin came off
when he removed his socks.

Spyros studied at Jones Commercial College for
two years. Later he took night courses at the Benton
College of Law, because he understood the value of
commercial law in the business career which he
planned. During all this time he and his two brothers
lived frugally, walking to work to save the nickel
carfare and allowing themselves only an occasional
Sunday afternoon's entertainment at the nickel-
odeons, the precursors of our moving pictures.

By 1913 the three brothers had accumulated
$3500 in their joint bank account. Being approached
by three fellow Greek-Americans in search of capital,
they put up $3000 of their saving for a quarter in-
terest in a new nickelodeon called "The Olympia."
Soon, however, the new partners quarreled. The
Skouras brothers, who had invested their profits from
the new venture jointly, bought out the other three.
In a short while they were able to buy another small
theater. They were on their way to financial success
in the entertainment world.

Spyros had become a citizen of the United States
and, in 1917, with our country at war, he joined the
U.S. Air Force. He was trained as an aviation cadet,
but the war was over before he received his commis-

sion, and he saw no overseas service. Honorably discharged from the Air Force, he returned to St. Louis
and worked with his brothers upon the expansion of
their theater holdings. By 1926 the brothers had an
interest in almost every important St. Louis theater.
They built a $6,000,000 building in which to house
their Ambassador Theater, a showy movie palace of
the type that was soon to dominate the American
scene. After a brief war with Paramount, which
Spyros won by enlisting the aid of a former customer
at the Planters Hotel, they began nation-wide operations. The elaborate stage and screen shows that were
"the wonder of St. Louis" were soon being developed
by the Skourases in theaters throughout the country.

The hotel experience of the three brothers had
taught them the importance of courtesy and service. They discovered that the "personal touch" was
as important in a theater as in a hotel. As a matter of
fact, the two older brothers insisted upon treating
their customers so effusively that George, the junior
partner and man of all work, once rebelled. "Listen!"
he angrily told his brothers. "I will polish the brass. I
will carry the film. I will sweep with the broom. But,
by God, I won't smile all the time. My cheeks ache!"

Spyros, more pliant and affable than George, soon
became the spokesman for the brothers in dealing
with the public. Charles, the cautious patriarch, kept
Spyros' grandiose schemes in check and held the purse

strings. It was Charles who would decide when the family budget could stand the strain of new clothes, and it was he who led the expedition downtown for the purchase of three identical blue serge suits. It was Charles, too, who supervised the health of the group, insisting that his brothers consume quantities of fruit, cheese, olive oil, and yogurt, and working out with them regularly on the wrestling mat which he had installed in their quarters.

Charles's role as boss of the three brothers has often been exploited for economic reasons. A story is told of Spyros' having settled a contract with a film salesman for a high price. Upon conclusion of the deal, Charles walked into the office and was told of the cost. He immediately grew angry and shouted. "What! Spyros, you are trying to bankrupt us!" Spyros insisted that he had made a good deal, and the two brothers began to argue furiously. They pounded the table, tore open their ties, ripped their shirts, kicked the furniture, and shouted at the top of their voices, while the frightened salesman sat and watched.

Finally Charles screamed, "O.K. Mr. Skouras! I don't call you brother any more. Go back to Greece!" Then he charged from the office, slamming the door and breaking the glass.

Spyros, apparently overcome, turned to the quaking salesman and gasped, "See, I did my best." The salesman, thoroughly hoodwinked, signed a new contract with Spyros at a much lower figure. The episode, with minor variations, was frequently repeated.

Actually, of course, the brothers worked in close concert with one another. As a matter of fact, one of the secrets of their early business success was their interchangeability. At business meetings that sometimes lasted all day and half the night the brothers would often spell one another. With his opponents groggy from lack of sleep, one Skouras would slip out for a steam bath, a rubdown and a nap while, unbeknown to the weary antagonists, a brother replaced him and continued the negotiations.

The Skourases were hard hit by the financial crash of 1929, but they soon bounced back. They bought up a chain of theaters cheaply and were soon making money on them. Spyros took over a bankrupt chain of movie houses in the West, and within three years he had them on a paying basis again. He helped to reorganize the Fox Film Corporation, recommending the amalgamation which resulted in the formation of Twentieth Century Fox Pictures. Though Spyros gained nothing directly from this deal, the good will he won was important. In 1942 he was made president of the new film producing company. He continued to play an active role in the theater management end of the business until the antitrust division of the Department of Justice started its battle to separate the production and management functions of the film industry. When the dust of that battle settled, the legal connections among the Skourases were severed. But there was no severing the close family ties uniting Charles, heading 550 theaters comprising the second largest chain in the country, George, controlling seventy movie houses in the East, and Spyros, with a $250,000-a-year job as head of one of the largest film producing companies in the country.

Though Spyros Skouras sees over three hundred films a year and believes, according to a friend, that movies have been "the greatest civilizing influence since Christianity, the greatest educational influence since the invention of movable type, the greatest cultural advance since the age of Pericles, and the greatest agency for political stability since the Roman Empire," his own greatest contribution to civilization was made in a sphere far removed from that of the moving picture. It was he who was responsible for organizing and directing Greek War Relief when Italy and Germany invaded Greece and laid it waste in World War II. He helped to raise over $12,000,000 for food, clothing, and medical supplies for the sick and starving people of his native country. And he managed, in the face of an impossibly complex international situation, to get the warring countries involved in Greece to refrain from interfering with these supplies. In undertaking this enormous job, he acted purely from humane sentiments and not because of loyalty divided between the country of his birth and the country of his adoption. When he was told that a toast was to be proposed to King George of Greece at a luncheon he was to attend in London for Greek War Relief, he objected. "Tell them I don't want it," he said, "because I am an American."

Despite the drastic inroads that television has made upon moving-picture profits, Spyros Skouras continues to be one of the most highly paid executives in the entertainment world. Once a New York financier criticized him for taking too large a share of the profits in these hazardous times for the film industry. But in a battle for the financial control of Twentieth Century Fox Film Corporation, Skouras' critic was defeated.

The once impoverished Greek immigrant boy still nourishes boundless optimism and grandiose plans for the future. Financial retrenchment in the face of television competition and diminished audiences is unthinkable to him. Instead of cutting down expenses, he has committed the entire resources of his studios— an investment of $30,000,000—to a new widescreen film technique designed to give audiences an enormous panoramic picture and a new illusion of depth. Though Spyros' own slogan, "Movies Are Better Than Ever," may be optimistic, no one can say that they are not bigger than ever.

Dimitri Mitropoulos

W HEN Dimitri Mitropoulos came to New York in the winter of 1940 to be the guest conductor of the Philharmonic Symphony Orchestra, New York music lovers were thrilled with his performances. At his last concert at Carnegie Hall, a standing audience whistled and cheered until the conductor had returned to the platform ten times. The tall, craggy-featured musician was so overcome by the warmth of the reception that he suddenly bent over and kissed the astonished concert master, Michel Piastro. While the audience cheered, the reviewers rushed to their typewriters to tell the story of this new conductor, who looked like a quiet philosopher and had the energy of a dynamo. "It is clear that Mr. Mitropoulos is no conductor of ordinary caliber," said one critic. "He gave the audience of the Philharmonic Symphony more sensations to the square minute than it had experienced in months preceding," spurted another reviewer. The intense, energetic Greek had captured New York!

Dimitri Mitropoulos was born in Athens, Greece,

in 1896. His family was a devout one, firmly believing in the Greek Orthodox religion. As every father dreams for his son, Dimitri's father dreamed for his. He wanted the boy to become a monk. Dimitri's two uncles had joined such an order, and his grandfather was a priest in the Greek Orthodox Church. When the boy went to visit his uncles at their monastery, he, too, desired to become a religious. As he said later, "I was inspired by the beauty and the unworldliness of the surroundings." The atmosphere of simplicity —beauty apart from the outside world—appealed to the contemplative nature of the boy. From all indications he would have entered such an order had there not been an active conflict which interfered with his plans. The Greek Orthodox Church forbids the use of any musical instruments in religious services. Dimitri's musical talent was already sprouting and he could not bear to be deprived of music. Had he become a monk, his musical genius might have remained undeveloped and would have been denied to the world.

The philosophical serenity of Dimitri Mitropoulos' temperament was a dominant characteristic of the man. Like many famous men, his greatness came not only from his musical ability but from his deeply religious nature. A picture of him makes one think of a kindly friar. A tanned complexion makes his deeply set, blue eyes even more intense. His face has a calm, thoughtful look that makes one think that he is at peace with the world. His serenity inspires confidence, and at the University of Minnesota, where he lived in a small dormitory room during his first years in Minneapolis, he became an adviser to students on every conceivable subject. They went to him for help about problems ranging from love affairs to musical ambitions.

When Dimitri Mitropoulos was ten years of age, he had mastered the complete score of *Faust* and *Rigoletto*, two difficult operas. By fourteen he had memorized the scores of almost every opera in the standard repertoire. All his energies were centered around his piano. At that time he could not decide whether to become a concert pianist or a conductor. Dimitri's father was a merchant and not particularly musical. However, the father finally despaired of the din which his son created in the house and realized that the boy's enthusiasm for music could not be discouraged, so he sent Dimitri to the Athens Conservatory to study.

The rumblings of war between Greece and Bulgaria interrupted the young musician's concentrated study. He entered the army and was made a drummer in a military band. The martial drum beats were a far cry from the melodic operatic music that was so close to his heart and so much a part of his life.

At the end of the war Dimitri put aside his army

uniform and went to the University of Athens to continue his studies. Here, while still in his early twenties, he wrote his own opera, *Sister Beatrice*. It was so successful that the directors of the Athens Conservatory decided to give it a special production. Luck that night was sitting right next to Dimitri Mitropoulos, for in the audience was the famous French composer, Camille Saint-Saëns. The Frenchman was so impressed that he arranged for scholarships and before long Dimitri set out for Berlin to study with the great composer Ferruccio Busoni. Here he quickly proved himself a capable musician; and, after he had completed his studies, he was appointed assistant conductor at the famous German State Opera House, the Berliner Staatsoper. The job of assistant conductor is a dreary one of training the orchestra until the day of the performance, when the conductor himself takes over. But Dimitri was willing to serve the dreary apprenticeship as long as it gave him training and experience.

Athens was not going to allow its young conductor to wander abroad too long. In 1926 the Athens Conservatory offered him the position of permanent conductor of the Athens Symphony Orchestra. Mitropoulos went back to Greece, but he was not content to stay in one place. He was invited to conduct the Berlin Symphony. Later Paris was shouting for him to come and see what he could do with the Symphonique de Paris. Everyone wanted to hear the Greek who was doing such wonderful things with music.

By this time Mitropoulos' fame had spread to America. At the invitation of Serge Koussevitsky, the conductor of the Boston Symphony Orchestra, he came to the United States as a guest conductor. Old-line Bostonians at first looked down their noses at the idea. Their cold reception was to thaw considerably, however. When Mitropoulos made his debut, his ability to make music memorable left the audience cheering. His success in Boston echoed as far west as Minneapolis, and Dimitri Mitropoulos was invited to become permanent conductor of the Minneapolis Symphony Orchestra. Almost singlehandedly, he transformed the once mediocre Minneapolis Symphony into one of the best orchestras in the country. His concerts in the impressive Northrop Auditorium on the campus of the University of Minnesota attracted what was said to be one of the largest single regular musical audiences in the United States. When he left Minneapolis in 1949 to become musical adviser for the New York Philharmonic Society, he was greatly missed by Midwestern concert goers. But Minneapolis' loss was New York's gain. As conductor and musical director of the New York Philharmonic Orchestra, he was a great success.

But what was it about this musician that made him such a wonderful conductor? Perhaps some of his ability may be attributed to the great sensitivity of his nature. His body was like a well-strung, expertly tuned musical instrument that responded to each note played upon it. The men who worked with him said that the intensity of his feeling made his eyes almost hypnotic and that he seemed to be everywhere in the orchestra, demanding the tones that he wanted from each instrument.

While more conservative music lovers may have frowned at the gymnastics in which Mitropoulos indulged when he directed, no one doubted his sincerity. He was eager to have perfection, and his whole body reacted against notes that were off-key, no matter how slightly. While he was conducting, his hands would cut little figures in the air like tiny sound shapes. One finger would pick out an instrument he wanted to emphasize, a swooping of his wrists would bring up one section of the orchestra, or with his wrists pulled up into his sleeves his body would quiver with the impact of the orchestra's sound. He knew exactly what he wanted to hear, and, what's more, he got it! The result was beautiful music.

Dimitri Mitropoulos is a man of remarkable memory. At his first rehearsal with the New York Philharmonic Symphony Orchestra he delighted the 101 members by naming most of them from memory. He could refer back to any passage in a score without looking back at the sheet. As he said, "I wouldn't like to see an actor playing *Hamlet* from a book. I learn the music." And so he did! When he was on the platform, there was no effort to remember the score. It came easily, and he seemed to be able to hear every instrument in the orchestra, and to know every note it was supposed to be playing. Since he did not use a baton or a score, he was free to concentrate on the music alone.

Temperamental fits, which are supposed to be common among musicians, were never indulged in by Mitropoulos. Neither did he give tyrannous scoldings to his men. He made them work hard, it is true, but he commanded their respect—a respect which bordered on devotion. For example, the Boston Symphony Orchestra is always considered one of the most hard-boiled musical organizations, but during one rehearsal with Dimitri Mitropoulos the entire orchestra put down its musical instruments and applauded. What greater tribute to a musician than to be so honored!

Much to the distress of the society matrons of Minneapolis, Mr. Mitropoulos preferred to spend his afternoons seeing Wild West movies rather than attending social teas. He was solitary by nature and loved to tramp off by himself to the mountains. Once, while flying over Alaska, he found his cherished dream—a tiny island lost in a broad lake. "Someday I shall retire and go up there to live in quietness," Mitropoulos remarked when he saw it. His one-time wish to become a monk never quite left him.

In spite of his love for solitude, Mr. Mitropoulos' kindness attracted many people to him. His generosity is almost a legend around Minneapolis. Insisting that $3000 a year was plenty for him to live on, he spent the rest of his money helping three students through college. He was always willing, too, to aid aspiring young musicians who were not so fortunate or so experienced as he was. One time a young man came to Dimitri Mitropoulos with his music. The conductor almost reduced the young musician to tears by telling him how bad the score was. Then he offered to pay the aspiring composer's tuition for an advanced course in composition at the University of Minneapolis.

Dimitri Mitropoulos was not only a great musician; he was also a great man. And in the tradition of the great man, he died with his boots on, as it were, succumbing to a heart attack during an opera rehearsal in Milan, Italy, where he was appearing as a guest conductor, on November 3, 1960.

Judith Anderson

O N February 10, 1898, in Adelaide, South Australia, half a world away from the bright lights of Broadway which would one day blazon forth her name, Judith Anderson was born. Life was harsh in the island continent down under the equator, and passions flared hotly there, but Judith and her three older brothers and sisters were cushioned from shocks during their early years by the soft bolster of wealth. Their father, an enterprising Scotsman named James Anderson-Anderson—Judith later shortened the double barreled name for the stage—had made a great deal of money in the undeveloped land, and he and his English wife lived well. There was a fine house with servants, and the children were sent to expensive private schools. Judith studied at Rose Park during her early years and later attended the exclusive Norwood School.

But changes were rapid in that pioneer country, and before Judith had finished school her father's fortune was wiped out and the family was reduced to near poverty. The economic distress seemed all the more acute by contrast with the luxury of earlier years. With the protective insulation of wealth stripped away, the violence and passion of life were revealed to the observant young Judith for the first time. Having studied dramatics at school, she yearned to express the emotions which she saw blazing around her in the raw new towns with whose inhabitants she now began to mingle.

Judith Anderson soon found an outlet for her ambition in a provincial Australian theater. As her talents developed, she was given increasingly difficult roles. In 1915 she won the important role of Stephanie in *A Royal Divorce,* establishing herself as a mature actress at the age of seventeen. Then for three years she toured the country with a traveling stock company, playing in most of the larger Australian cities. Despite her success with this company, however, Miss Anderson was not satisfied. The Australian theater was small and undeveloped. Moreover, the young actress had heard rumors of marvelous opportunities and fabulous salaries far across the wide Pacific in the fast-growing city of Hollywood, where the American moving-picture industry was rising. So in 1918, armed with letters of recommendation from Australian theater managers and accompanied by her mother, Miss Anderson left Australia, bound for California and a career in the moving pictures.

Hollywood proved disappointing to the young actress. No one there had ever heard of the important people who praised her talent in glowing letters of recommendation. She was told that she was too thin for the movies. Producers, accustomed to the soft prettiness of Hollywood stars, looked askance at her harsh features. Thin-lipped, hawk-nosed, and with deep-set, smoldering eyes, she was nothing like the conventional bright-eyed, well-powdered, empty-headed Hollywood ideal of feminine beauty. Directors, obsessed with this vacuous ideal, failed to discern the passion which animated Judith Anderson's young frame. They considered her awkward, and she looked in vain for a job.

After many months spent in fruitless visits to the studios, where she was interviewed, screen-tested and rejected time after time, Miss Anderson decided to leave Hollywood and try her fortune in New York. Perhaps in the more perceptive world of the legitimate theater her talent would be recognized. At least it would be worth trying, and something had to be done soon, for the Andersons' cash was running low. So Judith and her mother packed up their few belongings, purchased tickets out of their dwindling supply of cash, and headed for New York.

In Manhattan they had no better luck at first. To most New Yorkers Australia simply meant kangaroos. Judith's early success in her native land was of little interest to them. But the young girl was determined to be an actress. She haunted the offices of the booking agents, refusing to give up the idea of a career in the theater even after her money had run out. She and her mother moved to shabbier and shabbier rooming houses, living on next to nothing and paying their rent out of the few pennies that Mrs. Anderson, an inexperienced seamstress, was able to make by taking in sewing.

Eventually fatigue and undernourishment took their toll of Judith's health. An influenza epidemic swept New York that winter and she succumbed to the disease. Before she had thoroughly recovered from her illness, she was out tramping the streets again, searching for a part in a play. She made the rounds of the booking agents and was about to return to the dingy room in which her mother had nursed her through her sickness. Suddenly, a wave of giddiness swept over her and, stepping back into an office, she fell down in a faint.

That faint was the beginning of her American theatrical career. The manager of the Fourteenth Street Stock Company was in the office in which Miss Anderson collapsed and, motivated by pity for the young girl's condition and admiration for her pluck, he offered her a job. There was to be no nonsense about gratitude, he insisted. He needed someone to play supporting roles in his company, and he was willing to try out Miss Anderson. The salary was forty dollars a week, out of which the actress had to supply appropriate clothing for the roles she would play.

At the prospect of making forty dollars a week Miss Anderson was overjoyed. Her costumes could be made by her mother, thus enabling her to stretch her salary. Cleaner, less depressing rooms would be found. Food would be more plentiful. And, best of all, she would be back in the theater again.

The smell of grease paint was like a tonic to the young actress and, soon, her health restored and her self-confidence renewed, she was promoted to bigger roles, getting a ten-dollar increase in salary. In 1920 she toured the country in *Dear Brutus,* playing opposite William Gillette. Other leading roles followed. And in 1924 she enjoyed her first Broadway triumph, as Elise Van Zile in *Cobra.* The play was not a very promising vehicle for a young star to establish a reputation with. But Miss Anderson, with the magic of a great actress, made her audiences forget the limitations of the play. Commenting on her performance, one critic said, "She made this rather shoddy melodrama into a vibrant and unforgettable thing." And almost everyone who saw her was equally enthusiastic.

Judith Anderson had arrived.

Her success in *Cobra* brought Miss Anderson an offer from David Belasco, the theatrical impresario. Starring in *The Dove* for him, she was so successful that the play ran for two seasons. When it closed, the actress decided to revisit Australia, where she re-enacted her successful role in *Cobra*. On that visit she also acted in *Tea for Three* and *The Green Hat*. Then, returning to America, she successfully created the first of her many evil women, playing the part of the worthless rich woman in *Behold the Bridegroom*.

In 1928 Eugene O'Neill's Pulitzer Prize play, *Strange Interlude*, was produced in New York under the auspices of the Theater Guild. The unconventional play was a difficult one to stage. Its nine long acts could be unbearably tedious with careless or uninspired actors. Moreover, O'Neill had written scenes in which the characters speak their thoughts aloud while the other actors pretend not to hear them. Unless these speeches were skillfully presented, the results would be ridiculous. Lynn Fontanne, one of America's finest actresses, was selected by the Guild to play Nina, the difficult female lead. Miss Fontanne played the part with some success, but after a short run she withdrew from the play. Judith Anderson was selected to take her place. She faced tremendous obstacles: the difficult part had to be learned in a short time; she would be working with a veteran cast unfamiliar to her; a relative newcomer to the American stage, she was replacing a star with an international reputation. Furthermore, O'Neill's dramatic experiment was attracting much attention and some criticism as a radical artistic innovation. Despite these terrifying conditions, Miss Anderson took the part. Her interpretation astounded the spectators, and critics who came to mock the substitute remained to congratulate the star. She played the role to loud acclaim, overshadowing her distinguished predecessor in the part. And after an extremely successful season, she went on an extended tour with the play.

Having established the fact that she was capable of interpreting works of literary importance as well as more popular plays, Miss Anderson turned next to the experimental drama of Luigi Pirandello, playing the part of the Unknown One in *As You Desire Me* during 1930 and 1931. In the latter year she also undertook the role of Lavinia in O'Neill's *Mourning Becomes Electra.* The central character of the famous trilogy, Lavinia is O'Neill's counterpart to the Electra of the Greek dramatists. Miss Anderson had the difficult task of making the legendary Greek heroine credible in the light of Freudian psychology, for O'Neill conceived the tragedy as "a modern psychological drama using one of the old legend plots of Greek tragedy." Already a distinguished interpreter of O'Neill, Judith Anderson's success in the role marked her as one of America's foremost actresses.

During the three years following her triumph in *Mourning Becomes Electra,* Miss Anderson enjoyed less spectacular successes in less important plays. *Firebird,* in which she appeared in 1932, and *Conquest,* a 1933 vehicle, were entertaining stage plays but not great theater. Similarly, her next three plays, *Come of Age*, *The Female of the Species*, and *Divided by Three*, lacked the depth which a great tragic actress could exploit. However, in 1935 Miss Anderson was given a meatier part. Playing Delia, the strong sister in Zoë Aiken's Pulitzer Prize play *The Old Maid*, the actress won new laurels. And in the following year she was chosen by John Gielgud to play Gertrude in his *Hamlet*. Finally, having crossed the Pacific to triumph on the American stage, she crossed the Atlantic in 1937 for her first London appearance, winning an international reputation by her performance as Lady Macbeth. Later, when she played the same part in New York opposite Maurice Evans, Brooks Atkinson, the drama critic of the *Times*, called her acting "magnificent." Her Lady Macbeth, he said, "is strong without being inhuman. And she has translated the sleepwalking scene into something memorable; the nervous washing of the hands is almost too frightening to be watched."

Miss Anderson was married to Benjamin Harrison Lehman in 1937, but the marriage lasted only two years, culminating in divorce in 1939. Later that year she returned to Broadway in an unusual role. Portraying Mary, the mother of Christ, in *Family Portrait*, "She was," in the words of one critic, "all motherhood, without sentimentality."

Fresh from her triumph in O'Neill's *Mourning*

Becomes Electra, Judith Anderson had returned to Hollywood briefly in 1932. While there she had played "a sort of fuzzy gangster's moll in a thing called *Blood Money.*" She had hated it, and she vowed never to return to the movie colony. But in 1940 Alfred Hitchcock induced her to go back for a part in *Rebecca,* his first American film. Her characterization of Mrs. Danvers, the malevolent housekeeper in that picture, was so fine that she was asked to sign a seven-year contract with Metro-Goldwyn-Mayer. Excited by her recent film success, she agreed. Unfortunately, tense, rich, meaty parts like the one she had played in *Rebecca* were rare in Hollywood, and she didn't often get a chance to show what she could do as an actress. But not even another gangster role, in *Lady Scarface,* could dampen her enthusiasm for the new life she found. She enjoyed being up at dawn and in the studio from 6:45 in the morning to 7 at night. She liked the climate of Southern California. And after years of trouping, she appreciated the opportunity to settle down in one place.

Returning to New York on a brief visit after she had signed her seven-year movie contract, Miss Anderson amazed veteran Hollywood-beat reporters by arriving with a single suitcase. And they were flabbergasted when she announced by way of explanation, "I've got no interest in clothes. . . . I've got to save my money to buy fertilizer and seeds." The reason for her concern was soon apparent, for she could talk of nothing but her new "baby"—a house and three acres of land at Pacific Palisades. "For years I lived in trunks, suitcases and railroad stations," she said, "and now I've bought a house. I'm a sleepy, lazy girl, and I love the earth. I love the space. I love the sunshine. I love the trees."

On her California estate, Miss Anderson abundantly enjoys these beloved things. Much of her free time is spent out of doors, where she loves to romp, hatless, with her two dachshunds. Her leisure is also occupied with the cultivation of her garden and the decoration of her beautiful house. Though she appreciates privacy and, according to newspaper columnists, "cannot be interviewed," she is no recluse, brooding morosely in solitude, as many of her stage and screen roles might lead one to assume. A gourmet, she gives delightful dinner parties for an intimate circle of friends. A rich vein of humor runs through her personality, and her friends maintain that she has "a talent for gaiety." Indeed, her characteristic expression of interest is a low chuckle that seems to be the result of sympathetic communion with an internal confidante. And her interest is aroused by people of all sorts, being stimulated by their inner make-up and thoughts rather than by their external characteristics.

Miss Anderson gave amply of her personal warmth

and rich humor during World War II. Heading a USO unit, she toured the battle areas of the South Pacific, entertaining troops in forward combat zones with scenes from Shakespeare and other dramatists. Her group was one of the first units with a top-flight star to visit forward battle areas, one of the few units that attempted to bring beauty and dignity as well as laughter to the fighting men. A sailor who saw the show in New Guinea said later, in a *Collier's* article called "Shakespeare on the Jungle Circuit," that it was "a rare and wonderful show" with a special sort of atmosphere "provided largely by Judith Anderson's own warmth, and sincerity, and honesty."

After the war Miss Anderson, who had remarried in 1946, returned to the theater again. And in Robinson Jeffers' free adaptation of Euripides' *Medea* she reached the pinnacle of her career. Describing her performance, a New York drama critic wrote:

> No dynamo could surpass her in energy. As she moves up and down the steps of the palace her body is always at the command of her emotions. She uses gestures that are large, bold and varied. Her arms speak a language of their own. Her voice, which is uncommon both in its range and timbre, can wheedle, plead, accuse, or mock. At one moment it crackles like a roaring fire from passion's heat. At the next it hisses like a pit full of snakes.

Medea was called "a performance of a scale, freedom and kind that Miss Anderson alone of present-day actresses could give." A theatrical event of the first magnitude, Miss Anderson's *Medea* will be cherished in the memory of the fortunate audiences that saw it.

Robinson Jeffers had dedicated his adaptation of *Medea* to Judith Anderson. When the poet wrote *The Tower Beyond Tragedy* he remembered her face, "dark, hawk-like, with black, burnt-out eyes, like a mask of despair," and he created the part of Clytemnestra especially for her. In 1951, when she played the role in New York, critics, already convinced that she was "the one modern player unashamed of the glories of her craft," had to look back to the great French tragedienne Rachel to find a fitting standard by which to judge her ability. "She is the panther of the stage," they said. "With a panther's terrible beauty and undulating grace she moves and stands and glares and springs. Scorn, triumph, rage, lust and merciless malignity she represents in symbols of irresistible power." Miss Anderson's long specialization in evil parts, which were in essence little more than character parts dignified by the intensity of her performance, had helped her to perfect her dramatic skill. In *Medea* and *The Tower Beyond Tragedy* she rose beyond evil as an expression of character to the tragic heights upon which terror is transformed by passion, apotheosizing the character who is caught up in its awful toils.

Miss Anderson had—and still has—other victories

to win. At the peak of her powers she demonstrated her versatility by participating in a theatrical experiment in company with Charles Laughton, Tyrone Power, and Raymond Massey. The experiment, which Miss Anderson described as "pure theater with no trappings of costume and scenery," was the dramatization of Stephen Vincent Benét's epic poem of the Civil War, *John Brown's Body*. Dressed in immaculate evening clothes, the four principals stood on a bare stage before an acting bar—a three foot high wooden railing on which the actors leaned, sat or slouched—and took turns reciting the narrative. In addition, each actor spoke the lines of a number of characters in the piece, Miss Anderson portraying the various female characters with marvelous facility, being now the lovely Sally Dupré, now naïve Melora, and now the strong-willed old plantation mistress. Foregoing the usual New York opening, the group made a tour of sixty American cities in twenty-eight states. Bringing "live drama to people all across the land," they reached and wrung the vitals of the country with their remarkable presentation. The experiment was a tremendous success.

The possessor of an unusual talent, Judith Anderson has demonstrated that she is no mere character actress specializing in evil roles. An actress of genius, she brings the entire force of her unique personality to bear upon any role she undertakes. Her full, rich, rather low-pitched voice is a flexible instrument upon which she plays with wonderful skill. But her voice is not the only instrument which she uses in interpreting a part. Her arresting face with its dark, haunting eyes is an extraordinarily mobile conductor of emotion. Her arms and hands twist in rage and anguish, jerk spasmodically with fear, or twine sinuously around a lover. Indeed, her whole body, alive with fluid grace, whirls or glides or springs with the sureness and beauty of a jungle cat. Miss Anderson speaks with the authority born of mastery of dramatic technique. And when she speaks, she speaks not with her lips alone but with her face, her arms, her body, revealing to her adopted countrymen a world of beauty and terror rarely seen upon the modern stage.

Alfred Hitchcock

Scene: A merry-go-round in an amusement park. Gay carousel music. Laughter. Children scampering about, choosing their favorite wooden horses for the ride that is about to begin.

Lights!   Action!   Camera!

A whirl of brightly colored horses round and round. Suddenly, guns blaze. The operator of the machine is hit and his carousel circles madly, out of control. Men run into the spinning circle, exchanging shots amid a swirl of screaming children and lunging wooden horses, while the music pipes gaily away.

Cut!   Stop the cameras!

The scene is marked by the unmistakable "Hitchcock touch," its carefully detailed background of gaiety counterpointing the stark horror of the action of the unfolding plot.

But let's follow the swinging boom of the camera to another imaginary set, for it is not alone in such dramatic contrasts as we see illustrated in this scene from *Strangers on a Train* that the Hitchcock touch consists. It is rather in the skillful use of the camera to pick up and emphasize details significant for his purpose that Hitchcock excells. Observe, for instance, the classic example of fine camera work from the film *Foreign Correspondent*.

We are looking down from a balcony into a crowded, rain-drenched square. Beneath their glistening umbrellas, thousands of people stand, waiting expectantly for the appearance of a distinguished statesman. There is a flurry of activity as the famous man steps from a building. Photographers, shielding their cameras from the rain, kneel on the wet stones to photograph him. Bang! A shot sounds. The great man slumps to the ground. Dead. An enemy agent disguised as a photographer, his gun concealed in a camera, has assassinated the statesman. Now, from the vantage point of the balcony, we watch the agent's escape, his path revealed from above as our camera follows a disturbance through the mass of densely packed, glistening umbrellas.

Our position has enabled us to observe the escape. But more than that, it has pointed up the difficulty of detecting the fleeing man amid the obstacles at the scene of action. Again, the Hitchcock touch!

Having seen Hitchcock at work, let us use our make-believe camera for a flashback. The scene is London. The time, August 13, 1899. We are in the crowded, noisy streets of a market district. Our camera, panning, reveals stalls heaped up with fruits and vegetables and butcher shops with the bloody carcasses of slaughtered animals hanging in the windows. It comes to rest upon a sign:

WILLIAM HITCHCOCK, POULTERER

Inside the store beneath this sign the proprietor is weighing a freshly killed chicken for a customer. He pauses nervously, looking over his shoulder toward the back of the shop. Then he finishes his job and walks to the rear of the store. Opening a door, he listens expectantly. In a moment there is a loud wail from the upper story and William, still wearing his stained shop apron, dashes up the stairs. In the hall above he is met by an elderly woman who informs him that his wife Emma has given birth to a husky baby boy. Alfred Hitchcock has just been born.

Young Alfred grew up amid the noise and color of the London market district in which he was born. He was an independent child with a craving for adventure, and he soon began to roam far from home in his search for it. Before he had reached his eighth birthday he had ridden to the end of every bus line in sprawling London. And when, during his boyhood, his father became a fruit importer as well as a poultry dealer, Alfred began to dream of still more distant places as he helped to unpack the exotic fruits that came to the store from the far corners of the world. He visited the London wharves and the ships set him dreaming of adventures in strange lands. One wall of his bedroom he covered with a huge map of the world. On it he traced the courses of British vessels through the seven seas, getting his information from shipping reports in the daily papers. Already he was displaying that interest in adventure and in exact detail that was later to distinguish his films.

While at St. Ignatius College, the London secondary school which he attended, Alfred decided that he wanted to become an engineer. Upon graduating, he enrolled at London University, majoring in electrical engineering. Soon, however, he had to quit the university, for his father's business was failing and Alfred had to help support the family. His training helped secure him a job as a technical clerk in a London cable manufacturing company. Abandoning any idea of becoming an engineer, he nevertheless continued his education, studying economics and art at night. His developing artistic talent soon made him a valuable asset to the company for which he worked, and he was advanced to the advertising department. Designing advertising layouts by day and attending school at night, young Hitchcock satisfied his craving for adventure by spending his odd moments at the newly invented moving pictures.

Though Hitchcock soon became an avid movie fan,

he was annoyed by the inartistic way in which the film titles were announced on the screen. The sloppily executed list of credits also disturbed him. Using the titles of some of the films he had seen and filling out the list of credits with the names of friends, Hitchcock designed a series of title and credit cards that were artistically satisfying. Presenting himself at the newly opened London studios of the Famous Players Company, Hitchcock ran the gamut of doorkeepers, secretaries, and vice-presidents with his cards. Eventually he reached the head of the film company, who liked his ideas so well that he hired Hitchcock immediately, putting him in charge of the title department of the Famous Players Company. The year was 1920. Alfred Hitchcock's career in the moving picture industry had begun.

Hitchcock's first step toward the director's chair was taken a year or so later when he left the Famous Players Company for a job with Gainsborough Pictures. As a matter of fact, his new position with the smaller company involved several jobs, for he functioned as art director, script writer, assistant director, and production manager. But he was soon a full-fledged director, and it was in that capacity that he made his reputation, producing for Gainsborough, and later for Gaumont-British Films, moving pictures which helped put the British film industry on its feet.

One of the earliest films to reveal the authentic Hitchcock touch was a silent picture that he directed in 1926. Called *The Lodger,* it was a melodrama based on the exploits of Jack the Ripper, a notorious London murderer. In this picture Hitchcock used for the first time a device that was later to be identified with his name and that he himself came to consider "the core of the movie"—the chase. Skillfully employed, the chase gathers momentum in the picture as the terrified public and the police accumulate information that narrows the mysterious killer's sphere of operations. The action is largely psychological in the early reels, for the murderer is still unknown. But in the final reel, after a climax of tension has been reached, pent-up emotions are released in the swift movement of headlong flight and pursuit.

In *The Ring,* a silent film about a prize fighter which Hitchcock made in 1927, new film techniques that were to be exploited later with great success were introduced by the director. In one scene, for instance, the camera focuses upon a champagne glass in which the bubbly wine gradually goes flat while the elated young boxer waits in vain for his missing wife to return and celebrate his victory with him. The significance of the scene is thus revealed through the photography and not solely by means of dialogue or description, methods more appropriate in the theater and the novel.

Hitchcock called *Blackmail,* a picture which he made in 1929, a "silent talkie." Planned as a silent film with a view to conversion should the "talkies" prove to be practical, the sound was dubbed in after the picture was finished. The film was Hitchcock's first attempt at a "talking picture." In it he proved that the moving picture could assimilate human speech, the vehicle of the drama, without slavishly imitating the methods of the stage. He preserved the integrity of the film by continuing to emphasize the functional role of the camera.

For a time Hitchcock's principal interest lay in the adaptation of plays and novels to the screen. His most notable success with a filmed play was his movie version of Sean O'Casey's *Juno and the Paycock,* in which Barry Fitzgerald starred. Among the novels which he converted into movies were *Jamaica Inn,* starring Charles Laughton, and Hall Caine's *The Manxman.* These efforts helped pave the way for his skillful adaptation of Daphne Du Maurier's *Rebecca* into a film which won the Academy Award in 1940. His experiments convinced him, however, that the crime or spy melodrama provided the type of story that was best suited to the motion picture. His later films— with several striking exceptions—were largely confined to the exploitation of such stories.

Between 1935 and 1938 Hitchcock directed a cycle of six melodramas for Gaumont-British Films which have been described as "unquestionably his best work." These films were *The Thirty-Nine Steps* (based on John Buchan's thrilling story, *The Man Who Knew Too Much*), *The Secret Agent, Sabotage, The Girl Was Young,* and *The Lady Vanishes.* Of uniform excellence, these pictures are still being shown as outstanding examples of film art. Commenting on the cycle, Lawrence Kane in *Theatre Arts* analyzed Hitchcock's distinctive contribution to the screen in the following words:

> The Hitchcock style could at last be clearly defined. It resulted in melodramas told against painstakingly realistic backgrounds, taut of plot and characterization. His cameras moved with sureness and suddenness rarely equalled. His lighting retained only the best of what the German innovators had developed in the last decade, stark but never sensational for its own sake. He had achieved that most difficult of ends: the construction of a believable world from insubstantial shadow.

Hitchcock's success in creating a believable world out of insubstantial shadow is largely the result of his painstaking attention to detail. Together with his wife Alma, whom he married in 1926 when she was serving as his script writer and associate director, he plans out his scripts very carefully, hoping to follow them exactly when he starts to shoot. "In fact," says Hitchcock, "this working on the script is the real making of the film for me. When I've done it, the film is already finished in my mind."

The amount of effort that Hitchcock puts into a film before he begins to shoot can be illustrated by a comparison. The normal shooting script for a Hollywood movie consists of about fifty master scenes. A typical Hitchcock script is broken down into approximately six hundred numbered scenes, each complete with sketches of characters as they are to be grouped and with camera positions carefully noted. In addition, Hitchcock often furnishes the actors with dozens of his own lively sketches, illustrating the facial expressions he expects of them at various points in a scene.

It is not merely the amount of preparatory work, however, that determines the excellence of Hitchcock's best films. It is the result of the man's vision, of the appropriate use of means to secure a desired end. The procedure is best described in his own article, "Direction by Hitchcock" in *Footnotes to the Film,* when he says:

> What I like to do always is to photograph just the little bits of a scene that I really need for building up a visual sequence. I want to put my film together on the screen, not simply to photograph something that has been put together already in the form of a long piece of stage acting. This is what gives an effect of life to a picture—the feeling that when you see it on

the screen you are watching something that has been conceived and brought to birth directly in visual terms. The screen ought to speak its own language, freshly coined, and it can't do that unless it treats an acted scene as a piece of raw material which must be broken up, taken to bits, before it can be woven into an expressive visual pattern.

When the procedure suggested here is followed by a man of Hitchcock's talent, the results are such fine films as *The Thirty-Nine Steps, The Lady Vanishes,* and *Foreign Correspondent.*

Hitchcock's great British movies brought him offers from Hollywood and, after an exploratory trip to the United States in 1938, Hitchcock returned to take up permanent residence here, lured by a contract which offered him $800,000 for five pictures. *Rebecca* and *Foreign Correspondent,* his first American pictures, were as fine as his best British films. The former picture, adapted from a best seller, dealt with a theme different from those which Hitchcock customarily handled. But anyone who recalls the entrance of Mrs. Danvers, as played by Judith Anderson in that picture, will realize that the director had lost none of his skill. In explaining that scene Hitchcock says, "Mrs. Danvers . . . upsets you because she comes suddenly from nowhere right into your consciousness. Had I built her one of those stately pedestrian entrances, your reaction would have been at once, 'Oh, here comes the menace. I'm not scared a bit.' " The explanation shows that Hitchcock was still thinking of the acted scene "as a piece of raw material which must be broken up . . . before it can be woven into an expressive visual pattern."

Foreign Correspondent was a great spy melodrama that confirmed Hitchcock's reputation as a master of suspense. The hard-working director put so much effort into the filming of this picture that he lost over thirty pounds while it was being made. Enormously stout, Hitchcock didn't mind the weight loss. He still had over two hundred pounds left.

Up to this point in his career Hitchcock had not attempted a straight comedy. In 1941 he fulfilled his ambition to direct a typical American comedy about typical American people. The picture was called *Mr. and Mrs. Smith*. After producing it he returned to melodrama. But he was beginning to be affected by the unhealthy influence of the box office. His next picture, *Suspicion,* though it won an Academy Award for its star, Joan Fontaine, is marred by a compromise ending which destroys its artistic integrity. *Saboteur,* which Hitchcock directed in 1942, represents an attempt to cash in on his own reputation by imitating one of his early successes, *The Thirty-Nine Steps*.

Hitchcock redeemed himself somewhat in *Shadow of a Doubt,* a picture upon whose script he collaborated with the novelist Thornton Wilder. And his

directing of *Lifeboat* showed courage, for the strong-
est character in the film is a Nazi U-boat captain. But
his next three pictures reached depths of banality and
bad taste only equaled by veteran Hollywood hacks.
Spellbound, filled with conventional camera tricks,
was "immensely undistinguished from an artistic
point of view." *Notorious* was vulgar and trite. And
The Paradine Case was, according to one admirer of
Hitchcock, "the worst picture he ever made."

Unfortunately, the famous fat man, who trade-
marks his pictures by appearing briefly in each of
them, has not produced a picture recently that is
worthy of that famous stamp. Certainly none can be
identified without some such mark, however, for the
Hitchcock touch of earlier years is not in evidence
today. Indeed, the once-great director seems to have
refuted the principles upon which his early achievements were based. *Rope,* for instance, was shot a ten-
minute reel at a time instead of in the usual numerous
short takes. As a matter of fact, Hitchcock turned the
studio upside down in order to film continuous action
in long scenes. The result, as he might have expected,
is a thoroughly undistinguished picture. It could
hardly have been otherwise, for Hitchcock had long
ago said, "If I have to shoot a long scene continuously I always feel I am losing grip on it, from a
cinematic point of view. The camera, I feel, is simply
standing there, *hoping* to catch something with a
visual point to it." In *Rope* the camera hoped in vain.

In *Dial M for Murder,* Hitchcock once again adapted a stage play for the movies, and the adaptation relies heavily upon three-dimensional tricks of perspective and such devices as a prop telephone the size of a man. Nor does the telescope, through which Hitchcock focuses his camera in *Rear Window,* add significance to that slow-moving picture. Indeed, the director spends so much time emphasizing the importance of the telescope that he slows up the action of the film.

But it is time for us to leave our imaginary projection room, where we have been watching the career of Alfred Hitchcock, Director, unfold. Perhaps, with the increasing competition of television in the entertainment business, Hollywood film makers will soon be forced to re-examine their ideals. Should they do so, they may come to see that the medium of the film still has vast potentialities for those who approach it in the proper spirit, respecting the medium more than the large profits with which, heretofore, they have been almost exclusively concerned. If such a re-evaluation occurs, more films like *The Thirty-Nine Steps* will be seen. You will recognize them when you see them even if you miss the words "Directed by Alfred Hitchcock," or the scene in which the fat director appears briefly as a character. You will recognize them, for they will bear an unmistakable sign—the sure sign of the Hitchcock touch that also has achieved success on the TV screen.

Index

Adler, Felix, 89-97
  birth of, 89
  chairman of National Child Labor
    Committee, 95
  discussion of his ideals, 97
  as editor of *The Standard,* 97
  education and teaching of, 90, 96
  extracts from his *Ethical Philosophy
    of Life,* 92-93
  founder of Society for Ethical Cul-
    ture, 90-91, 93-94
  president of Eastern Division of
    American Philosophical Asso-
    ciation, 96
  quoted on education and child la-
    bor, 94-96
  reasons for break with Jewish faith,
    89-90
  writings of, 96-97
Agassiz, Louis, 10-19, 46
  Agassiz Museum, 16
  at Anderson School of Natural His-
    tory, 18
  anecdote about student life, 12
  awarded Legion of Honor, 15
  birth of, 10
  buried at Mount Auburn, 18-19
  chair of natural history at Law-
    rence Scientific School, 15
  *Contributions to the Natural His-
    tory of the United States,* 16
  education of, 10-12
  establishes reputation for research,
    12
  helps found national academy of
    sciences, 17
  injury to eyes, 13

Agassiz, Louis *(cont.)*:
  lectures at Lowell Institute, 14-15
  made member of Royal Society of
    London, 13
  obtains professorship at Neuchâtel,
    13
  opens his college courses to women,
    16
  opponent of Darwinian theory, 14
  plan for trip to Brazil, 18
  recipient of Wollaston prize, 13
  Researches on the Fossil Fishes,
    13-14
  teaching methods of, 16-17
  "The Prayer of Agassiz" (Whittier),
    18
  writes to Sir Philip Edgerton, 17
  as young naturalist, 10
  zoological collections, 16
American Academy of Fine Arts, 71
American Federation of Labor, 81,
    83-85, 87, 186
Anderson, Judith, 274-287, 297
  birth of, 274
  early dramatic yearnings, 275
  illness from influenza, 277
  marriage and divorce of, 281
  movies acted in, 282
  plays acted in, 275, 278-282, 284-
    286
  qualities as actress, 286-287
  settles in Pacific Palisades, 282-285
  signs contract with Metro-Goldwyn-
    Mayer, 282
  unsuccessful attempts in movies,
    275-276
  USO entertainer during war, 284